CULTURE OF OPPORTUNITY

CULTURE OF OPPORTUNITY

Obama's Chicago:
The People, Politics, and Ideas of
Hyde Park

Rebecca Janowitz

Ivan R. Dee   Chicago   2010

www.ivanrdee.com

Library of Congress Cataloging-in-Publication Data:
Janowitz, Rebecca, 1953–
    Culture of opportunity : Obama's Chicago : the people, politics, and
ideas of Hyde Park / Rebecca Janowitz.
        p. cm.
    Includes bibliographical references and index.
    ISBN 978-1-56663-833-3 (cloth : alk. paper)
    1. Hyde Park (Chicago, Ill.)—Social conditions. 2. Hyde Park
(Chicago, Ill.)—Politics and government. 3. Obama, Barack—Homes
and haunts—Illinois—Chicago. I. Title.
F548.68.H9J365 2010
977.3'1—dc22   2010001143

To Gayle and Morris Janowitz,
wonderful parents and exemplary citizens

CONTENTS

PREFACE

The Chicago neighborhood of Hyde Park has attracted unusual attention since Barack Obama's ascent to the presidency began. Many observers speculate about the community's contribution to his success. In telling this story, the advantage I have is two-fold: I began watching Hyde Park very closely more than forty years ago, and I have been an active participant in its community life.

Although I have served on the boards of various neighborhood organizations, the only group I ever led is the Fifty-seventh Street Children's Book Fair committee. That volunteer post, which I held on my own or in partnership for twenty-two years, afforded me a comprehensive introduction to Hyde Park's cultural and social scene. On the one hand, the neighborhood generously supported the venture. Individuals contributed wonderful ideas: Why not have a giant version of *Where's Spot?* so that a small child can actually walk into a favorite book? On the other hand, when we sent a college student dressed as Snow White to reward third-graders who had successfully struggled through summer school with gift sertificates for books, a local reporter criticized us for discriminating on the basis of academic achievement.

My interest in Hyde Park politics is long-standing. I have known many of the politicians and other public figures described in these pages. My political experience is at the grass-roots level and includes passing petitions, packing meetings, and watching polls. When Barack Obama once described me as a political person, I took it as a compliment.

Hyde Park has provided many people, including Obama, with unusual opportunities. I try to describe the political and social culture that produces these opportunities and how it developed. Hyde Park's culture is rooted in its history: decisions made fifty and a hundred years ago still shape the community.

My greatest regret about the book as it stands is the number of amazing Hyde Parkers who are absent from its pages. This reflects no lack of affection for them or respect for their accomplishments. But the goal here is a portrait of the neighborhood, not an encyclopedia.

I could not have completed this book without help from many friends. Jim Dispensa provided me with useful statistics on the public schools. Dori Jacobsohn helped me understand Gertrude Abercrombie. Toni Preckwinkle took time from the campaign trail, during her run for Cook County Board president, to answer my questions. Irene Sherr shared insights about Paul Cornell's work in the areas of parks and planning. Kenneth Sawyer patiently outlined the complex story of Hyde Park's numerous theological seminaries.

Oswelda Badal, Tara Baldridge, Jack Cella, Barbara Flynn Currie, Cydney Fields, Jackie Grimshaw, Philip Hanson, Prentiss Jackson, Bradley Jonas, Elizabeth Kirby, Ray Lodato, Rosa McCullagh, Sue Purrington, Sara Spurlark, and Mimi Zeltzerman generously shared personal experiences. Some read sections of the manuscript and offered thoughtful suggestions. Stephen Treffman read every chapter, caught many mistakes and acted as a coach and sounding board.

I owe special thanks to my mother, Gayle Janowitz, the kindest of copy editors, and Daniel Silverfarb, the severest of critics. My sons, Aaron and Daniel Collard, enrich my life every day and in different ways keep their father's spirit alive.

R. J.

Chicago
January 2010

CULTURE OF OPPORTUNITY

ONE
LIFE IN HYDE PARK

When Barack Obama won the 2008 presidential race, the staff of 57th Street Books hung a colorful hand-lettered sign in their small front window reading "Congratulations to Our Longtime Customer." 57th Street Books is a branch of Hyde Park's venerable Seminary Cooperative Bookstore, an independent business owned by its members. The Seminary Co-op has 54,000 members, 17,000 of whom live on the South Side of Chicago, and a worldwide reputation as a scholarly bookstore. Members have access to more than 230,000 volumes at the store's three locations in Chicago but cannot buy a cup of coffee at any of them. Hyde Park is an austere place. There is almost no nightlife. But the neighborhood has excellent facilities for writing books. An aspiring writer may buy paper, toner, and computers at

Office Depot, one of Hyde Park's handful of big box retailers. The would-be author may do research at numerous well-organized libraries and special collections. Once his or her book is published, a Hyde Park author hopes the senior staff of the Seminary Co-op will choose to place it on the prestigious front table. This local honor means a great deal to Hyde Parkers: the books on the front table are the best of the best, scholarly books expected to become classics and to influence thinking in more than one field.

The front table is located in the bookstore's main branch, the basement of a beautiful, dilapidated Protestant seminary. Customers enter through huge carved doors, pass through a medieval entryway, and walk down a steep staircase. One of the walls by the stairs is covered, as if by wall paper, with a vast and varied collection of posters and flyers announcing seminars, lectures, opportunities to participate in or object to research, and an endless array of protest meetings. The bookstore itself is made up of many small rooms, lined floor to ceiling with bookshelves, all arranged in a confusing pattern. The front table has its own place center stage in one of the first rooms. Almost everyone who comes into the bookstore pauses to check its contents. The front table does not have a sign; it has never needed one.

No president of the United States has shopped at the bookstore while in office. When President Clinton wanted to stop by, the Secret Service looked at the maze of tiny rooms and said no. The last time Barack Obama was spotted as a customer, he was a presidential candidate. He stopped by 57th Street Books with one of his daughters to help her find a book. His excited fellow customers yearned to speak to him but restrained themselves and sent all their friends breathless e-mails.

Nobel Prize winners, Supreme Court justices, famous scholars and writers, and thousands of serious readers belong to the Seminary Co-op. Like Obama, they all get careful attention

The window of 57th Street Books after Obama's presidential victory. Hyde Park celebrates its favorite son as a good customer.

from Jack Cella, the manager, who remembers what everyone reads and knows most of the books in the store. There is absolutely no parking available for anyone.

A Hyde Park author may benefit from a book signing party at 57th Street Books. Obama's first book signing there in 1995 drew a respectable thirty-five attendees. The second, in October 2006, which he loyally held at the same modest location, required the presence of police to control the crowds.

The author may get his or her hair cut or styled in Hyde Park, as the Obamas always did. If, however, the author needs an outfit to wear to the book signing, he or she will have to travel outside Hyde Park to buy a suit, or even a necktie.

Hyde Parkers understand that even a well-written book may not sell. Many serious new titles, the product of years of research and reflection, sell modestly. No one in Hyde Park would be surprised to learn that Obama's thoughtfully written and heartfelt first book, *Dreams from My Father*, was remaindered. Brad

Jonas, owner of Powell's Books, bought several thousand copies. For a while Jonas sold the books in his Hyde Park store. As a great admirer of Obama, Jonas offered him the copies during his 2000 campaign against Congressman Bobby Rush. He suggested they be given as gifts to donors and supporters. Obama insisted on paying for the books. Jonas was embarrassed to tell him that he had paid twenty-three cents a copy. Until *Dreams from My Father* was reprinted after Obama was elected to the Senate in 2004, Jonas supplied Obama and his campaigns with copies as needed. "If we got a call that CBS needed a copy, it went out special delivery."

Hyde Park–Kenwood, which includes the neighborhood immediately to the north, is an unusual place within the United States because it has achieved a rare stable racial balance. It is also economically diverse. While much of the population is middle class, wealthy people live in mansions and huge apartments near poor people living in subsidized units. Indeed, a DePaul University study recently identified Hyde Park–Kenwood as the most income-diverse community in Chicago. The study found that "high income households in Hyde Park (those earning $100,000 or more) account for 15.6 percent of its population, middle income for 37.8 percent, and low income for 46.5 percent." Thus Obama's imposing house is not located in a walled-off, uniformly affluent neighborhood. Poor Chicagoans can truthfully claim him as a neighbor.

The neighborhood carefully nurtures its children. The schools are good, and children can walk to them. The parks and playgrounds are plentiful and inviting. Sports programs are structured to avoid humiliating the inept. While academic competition is encouraged, too much pressure to succeed athletically is considered harmful to children. At least one Little League coach, asked each year to nominate children for the all-star

A young customer is off to a good start at the Fifty-seventh Street Children's Book Fair. (*Angela Sherrill*)

team, writes across the form, "All my players are stars" before returning it without nominations.

The Fifty-seventh Street Children's Book Fair brings unexpected whimsy and color to the street every September. Kids ride their bikes and explore a rich, culturally diverse world brought pleasantly to life in Blue Balliett's highly successful children's books. Hyde Park is now part of children's fantasies everywhere, and young readers walk into Powell's bookstore on Fifty-seventh Street looking for Balliett's fictional store owner or write to him at the store's address.

Hyde Parkers particularly exert themselves to bring the arts to children without dumbing down the content. They are willing to sacrifice their dignity to captivate a younger audience. At its annual Halloween concert, the University of Chicago Orchestra dresses in costume to play classical music. On one occasion the conductor, dressed as a genie, entered floating down the center aisle on a rolling cart topped by an Oriental rug. The concerts are packed.

Hyde Parkers have not been able to integrate all their public and private schools. St. Thomas the Apostle, the local Catholic church, prides itself on the diversity of its parishioners but runs an elementary school with an overwhelmingly black student body. It is not surprising that there are few black children at the Akiba Schechter Jewish Day School, which requires that students attending after kindergarten be Jewish. But parents at these schools and at those public schools with all-black student bodies know their children will have the opportunity to participate in integrated cultural and athletic programs and meet children of other races informally in the neighborhood.

The Chicago Children's Choir today includes more than 2,800 children throughout the city. The choir, interracial from the beginning, got its start in Hyde Park in 1956 in the First Unitarian Church. Many choir alumni remember that their experience under the guidance of founding director Christopher Moore was as important to them as their school days. The Hyde Park School of Dance, founded in 1993, provides classical ballet training for an interracial student body of more than 350, including a growing number of boys. Athletic teams such as soccer and Little League baseball include students from various schools and are diverse. At the same time special situations are carefully considered. When my sons were preparing for their bar mitzvahs, they were assigned to a soccer team with others in the same situation and scheduled only for early games on Saturday mornings. Thus they could dash into their classes with the rabbi, red faced and damp from a hasty shower.

Old people thrive in Hyde Park. It is safe and relatively clean, and cultural and educational activities abound. Many of the apartment buildings, both subsidized and market rate, have become naturally occurring retirement communities. Residents of the one planned retirement community have written a book about themselves. Age is openly respected, and difficult local residents are more loved as they age, whether or not they actually mellow.

Between the ages of twelve and eighty-two, however, Hyde Parkers are expected to produce and not pine for the bright lights of livelier urban places. Reminders of the need for rigor and focus abound. Students entering Kenwood Academy, the local public high school, as seventh-graders at the age of twelve or thirteen are proudly reminded that they attend the only Chicago public high school offering six years of Latin. More than 150 willingly enroll in Latin and compete for places on the school *certamen*, the team that represents the school in the Latin Olympics.

High productivity is expected in both paid and unpaid employment. Volunteers, whether working in the schools, parks, and cultural institutions or in political or protest campaigns, work incredibly hard. Some volunteer positions appear to be tenured. The requirements for volunteers are often high. People wishing to serve as docents at the University of Chicago's Oriental Institute, which displays Near Eastern artifacts, write qualifying papers in order to be allowed to explain hieroglyphs to schoolchildren. Newcomers to Hyde Park learn to never, ever dismiss anyone as just a volunteer.

This massive amount of unpaid labor provides extraordinary services to the community, particularly to its children. But the combination of volunteers and democracy can prove lethal to local institutions. In recent years, while the University of Chicago's Economics Department championed unfettered capitalism, the community's only large grocery store, a cooperative, died slowly as its volunteer board wrangled. A chain grocery store eventually arrived and prevented the neighborhood from joining the vast food desert that dominates much of the South Side, where there are often no real grocery stores.

The presence of 5,100 undergraduates at the University of Chicago (in addition to more than 10,000 graduate, professional, and other students, most of whom are not in the neighborhood), does not add much gaiety or dissipation to the community. The undergraduates cheerfully wear T-shirts that read "The University of Chicago: Where Fun Goes to Die." The punch line is, of course, that the students are proud there is so little fun to be had. Undergraduates may drink themselves into a stupor, but they rarely do it in public. When the university and the community enjoyed a moment of unity, cooperating to save Jimmy's, almost Hyde Park's only neighborhood bar, the emphasis was clearly on almost.

When Hyde Parkers gather to have fun it is often a complicated business requiring advance academic preparation. A perfect example is the annual Latke-Hamantaschen debate, a beloved, characteristically Hyde Park event sponsored every year by Hillel House, a Jewish organization on the university campus. The merits of a potato pancake versus a pastry are earnestly asserted by a panel of distinguished scholars, with tongues firmly in their cheeks, anxious to excel in the field of esoteric humor. The debates are so popular that it is difficult to get a seat. Hyde Parkers find it refreshing to hear famous academics make fun of themselves. The remarks are not off the cuff but painstakingly prepared in advance. Some have been published in a commemorative volume.

When the neighborhood gathers to pray, it is a lengthy business because of the inclusiveness required. On Thanksgiving morning, Hyde Parkers of all faiths gather in the University of Chicago's massive Rockefeller Chapel to offer thanks, listen to the neighborhood children sing, hear a sermon, and collect funds to feed the community's hungry citizens. Over the decades, the section featuring readings from the sacred texts of various faiths has grown from the original Protestant and Jewish to include Catholic, Hindu, Muslim, Buddhist, and Native American faiths. During the service, the congregants clearly articulate the kind of respectful, tolerant community they want to belong to and acknowledge the barriers to implementing their ideals in their city and nation.

Occasionally the neighborhood seems actively to fear pleasure. Former alderman and beloved political icon Leon Despres' last community campaign in 2009 was in support of voting a single Hyde Park precinct dry, a tactic once beloved by the temperance movement. The goal was to prevent demolition of an abandoned hospital and thereby stop the construction of a hotel to replace it. (The hotel could not operate profitably without a liquor license.) At times the neighborhood, so proud of stopping the demolition of Frank Lloyd Wright's Robie House and white flight, cannot seem to stop stopping things.

Hyde Parkers know that what happens in scholarly circles matters and can change the world. If they forget they do not live in an ivory tower, they can spend a few minutes looking at a hauntingly bleak sculpture by Henry Moore placed near the main university library. It marks the spot where on December 2, 1942, Enrico Fermi, winner of the Nobel Prize for physics and a recent refugee from Mussolini's Italy, achieved the first self-sustaining nuclear chain reaction using a pile of graphite bricks and uranium meticulously assembled in secrecy under an old squash court. More recently the theory of rational, self-adjusting markets, nurtured and oversold at the University of Chicago's Economics Department and Business School, brought substantial devastation to the world economy.

Hyde Park's puritanism, combined with the emphasis on families and children, suited the Obamas. Michelle's decision to plant a vegetable garden next to the White House and wear J.

Crew clothing reflect the style of Hyde Park. Her strength, of course, is that she sheds the Hyde Park style when appropriate.

Hyde Park is a comfortable place for wealthy and privileged people if they pitch in on community projects and are not too impressed with themselves. Consequently the wealthy people in Hyde Park are often hard to spot. Direct descendants of both Julius Rosenwald, who headed Sears, Roebuck, and Gustavus Swift, who founded the Swift meatpacking company, live in Hyde Park, but they blend in so well that a national press story recently concluded that they do not live there. No one pointed out that the article was wrong.

In a twist that is unusual in the United States, many of the wealthiest and most privileged people in the neighborhood are black. When I was a freshman at the University of Chicago's Laboratory High School in 1967, I remember that the school newspaper included the photos of four senior girls wearing formal evening dresses. They were all black and set to "bow," to make their social debut at the annual Links Cotillion. I do not recall any white girls in Hyde Park who had the social status to "bow" at a white debutante ball.

Black families that moved to Hyde Park in the late 1940s and early 1950s and have prospered have remained in the neighborhood, though they can afford to live elsewhere. South Kenwood is home to many grand mansions where wealthy blacks have lived, including Muhammad Ali.

Even less-affluent parts of the neighborhood have housed famous black people. In the 1960s Dick Gregory, the acerbic black comedian, lived in the University Park apartment complex on Fifty-fifth Street with his growing brood of children. Hyde Park has been a popular place for black musicians to live, from Ramsey Lewis to a host of less famous but talented individuals.

The neighborhood has enough affluent and well-connected black residents to create a substantial black elite. If these

Henry Moore's twelve-foot-high bronze *Nuclear Energy* marks the site of the world's first self-sustaining nuclear reaction at the University of Chicago. (*University of Chicago Library, Special Collections Research Center*)

residents dispersed in search of amenities they could afford else-where, they would constitute only a tiny fragment of any new community they joined.

During the summers of the late 1960s I joined other teenag-ers at the Hull House Music and Arts Camp in Wisconsin. Many children I knew from the neighborhood attended the camp. I also met many black kids from neighborhoods less affluent than Hyde Park and learned about hair relaxers and hot combs. The lives of poorer black kids were, however, already somewhat familiar to me from neighborhood programs I had attended or helped with from the time I was old enough to participate. For example, like many other Hyde Park children, including Arne Duncan, the current secretary of education, I began tu-toring early. By the time I was ten I was spending afternoons in a local "study center," a converted storefront, listening to a younger child read. The revelation for me at Hull House Camp was actually meeting a white working-class girl from Chicago and learning about *her* life. There were no white working-class neighborhoods adjacent to Hyde Park, and few working-class whites lived in the community. One of the white working-class neighborhoods closest to Hyde Park is Bridgeport, once home of Richard J. Daley, the present mayor's father and Hyde Park's chief political enemy during his tenure as mayor. In those years both black and white Hyde Parkers considered Bridgeport a hostile place, best avoided.

Interracial couples have long found Hyde Park a congenial place to live and raise their children. One newcomer to the neighborhood remarked that when picking up his child at Ray, a local elementary school, he learned to stop expecting parent and child to be of the same race. Today intermarriage is far more common everywhere in the country than even a few decades ago. But Hyde Park has more elderly interracial couples than most communities.

Occasionally there is friction around racial issues, but it tends to be petty. White people who feel that merely living in Hyde Park provides excellent left-liberal credentials can annoy their black neighbors. While white people who chose to live in the neighborhood sixty years ago were pioneers in building an interracial community, white people who live in Hyde Park today are not. At the same time wealthy black Hyde Parkers can grate on their less affluent white neighbors by focusing on the prejudice their children still face. White parents worried about paying for college do not want to hear about the rough time a well-to-do black freshman may still face at Yale.

Most white people want to live in Hyde Park if they grew up there, or prefer to live near the university. Otherwise white Chicagoans do not usually aspire to live in Hyde Park, which after all lacks shopping options, a movie theater, and other amenities.

Black people are more inclined to want to live in Hyde Park as a destination, apart from the university. The neighborhood has more amenities and is safer than most entirely black communities. Moreover white people, especially those outside Hyde Park, often cite safety as a reason *not* to live in Hyde Park while black people cite safety as a reason to live there.

Hyde Parkers of all races rely on the University of Chicago to ensure that their pleasant, culturally rich, oddly spartan lives are not disrupted by street crime. The university has maintained its own large police force since 1968. Before that it employed security guards. As violent crime, particularly related to drug dealing and gang activity, increased in Chicago during the 1960s and 1970s, the university stepped up its anti-crime efforts with considerable support from community members. Witnesses willing to testify in court were transported back and forth to hearings by university employees.

Today the university's police force numbers more than 140 officers with full arrest powers. University police officers attend the regular "beat meetings" held by the Chicago police as part of their community policing effort. Brightly lit call boxes that put a user in direct communication with the university police dot the neighborhood, and university students out for a late night party can call for a police escort to patrol the street as they walk home.

The University of Chicago Police now patrol neighborhoods outside Hyde Park–Kenwood, covering the area from Thirty-ninth Street to Sixty-fourth Street, and from Cottage Grove Avenue to Lake Shore Drive, in response to requests from residents of those communities for expanded patrols. People who are critical of the university, who for example believe that the university discriminates against black students and faculty, still want the university police patrolling their block.

The university police are seen as more concentrated on these specific neighborhoods than the city police. They are also seen as under stricter control than the city police. The university, it is assumed, does not want complaints about the conduct of its officers and would act swiftly to correct problems.

Interestingly, a black member of the University of Chicago faculty once suggested that the university disband its police force as an overture to the surrounding neighborhoods. It would have been an extremely unwelcome gesture as adjacent neighborhoods lobbied hard to get the university to extend the patrols to their streets.

For many years Rudy Nimocks, a black man who grew up on the South Side of Chicago, commanded the University of Chicago Police. Recently retired, Nimocks is a dapper, quietly self-confident man at ease with academics. He is a popular and well-respected authority figure in the community and in adjacent neighborhoods. Nimocks likes to tell people that he has lived at the same address in Woodlawn, a black neighborhood adjacent to Hyde Park, since 1952. He was always far better known and easier to reach than the various city police commanders who rotated through the two districts that include portions of Hyde Park.

The emphasis on publicly reporting crime has an unexpected downside. At least one well-intended group of residents recirculates the university's e-mailed crime alerts. The resulting plethora of warnings creates a classic "Google effect," convincing people that there is more crime than actually occurs. Now that the Secret Service has established a permanent presence in Hyde Park–Kenwood, guarding Obama's home, the neighborhood is even better protected as it confronts less crime.

The community's main grievances against the university have little to do with the police department. Instead they concern the University of Chicago Hospitals' unwillingness to provide much health care to the community. Another frequent criticism is that the university fails to manage its growing inventory of commercial properties effectively.

People with extreme views, or a history of extreme views, are tolerated in Hyde Park. For example, Elijah Muhammad, leader of the black separatist Nation of Islam, lived quietly for many years in a palatial Moorish-style home in South Kenwood near four smaller but substantial homes belonging to his sons. Louis Farrakhan, Elijah Muhammad's successor as head of the Nation of Islam, now lives in his mentor's former home. The streets surrounding the house are still patrolled by his guards, the Fruit of Islam. The neighbors feel that the presence of the Fruit discourages petty crime but complain that they take all the parking places. Apart from such minor grievances, the Black Muslim presence has never been a source for alarm. The vast majority of Hyde Parkers, black and white, disavow Farrakhan's beliefs, but as he never interests himself in purely local issues, they are not called upon to express opposition.

Farrakhan's house is only a few blocks from the headquarters of the Reverend Jesse Jackson's Operation PUSH. More Hyde Parkers would express a favorable opinion of Jackson than of Farrakhan. But on the rare occasions when Jackson has sought a direct role in Hyde Park politics, he has not been notably successful. Michael Johnson, principal of Reavis elementary school, was picketed by PUSH activists, but he is still principal. The alderman whose opponent Jackson supported is still in office.

William Ayers, the affluent, well-connected former leader of the radical Weatherman Underground, has lived in Hyde Park for years with his wife, Bernadine Dohrn, once also a prominent radical leader. The word "radical" is often used carelessly, but Ayers and Dohrn were certainly once worthy of the designation. They advocated the armed overthrow of the United States government and committed acts of violence in support of that goal. When they faced serious criminal charges they went underground. When they resurfaced, Ayers's wealthy family provided them with valuable assistance. For example, though

Dohrn pleaded guilty to serious charges, was placed on proba-
tion, later served jail time for refusing to testify against another
radical, and did not have a law license, she went to work at the
prestigious law firm of Sidley and Austin. Her employment was
arranged by Ayers's father, the former chief executive officer of
Commonwealth Edison, the major Chicago utility.

Ayers became a professor of education at the University
of Illinois at Chicago. Dohrn now works for Northwestern
Law School's Bluhm Legal Clinic. Their advocacy has become
quite genteel. Ayers criticizes public education in Chicago, and
Dohrn the juvenile court system. Neither has any direct personal responsibility for providing any indigent child with educational or legal services. Their work is praised and funded by
Chicago's political and philanthropic establishment, and neither
shows any sign of biting the hands that feed them.

Ayers and Dohrn have never stirred up controversy in Hyde
Park. They have avoided involvement in projects like the local
public schools or parks that are likely to produce differences of
opinion. They hosted a small fund-raiser for Obama when he ran
unopposed for the Illinois State Senate. Given their impeccable
upper-middle-class credentials and record of noncontroversial
advocacy for poor children, this raised no eyebrows in Hyde Park
at the time. When Obama ran for president, however, Ayers's
relationship with him became an issue. One of Ayers's neighbors
sent out an angry e-mail during the campaign responding to
attacks on Ayers. How could anyone criticize Ayers, the e-mail
asked, when he had coached a local Little League team?

In part this tolerance reflects provincialism. It also reflects
the understanding that people who hold extreme views can still
be of value to the community. A more important example than
Ayers is the Reverend Jeremiah Wright. Wright, who was always
a controversial figure, became a real problem to Obama during
his presidential campaign.

Unlike Ayers, Wright had a close relationship with Obama for many years. This was not unusual in Hyde Park. Long before Obama sought the presidency, Wright had many admirers among Hyde Park's well-educated black community who traveled forty blocks south to attend his church. If Wright ever took an interest in a local issue (and he has not), his direct influence within the community would far outweigh either Farrakhan's or Jesse Jackson's. Wright, who holds a master's degree from the University of Chicago's Divinity School, is both farther to the left and far better educated than many other prominent black ministers.

Wright created a significant option for well-educated young black people. His emphasis on social justice and his insistence that people should be proud to be African American inspired them. They found his willingness to discuss politics liberating as that subject is forbidden in many black churches. He deployed his formidable knowledge of the Bible and history to challenge them to think critically about important issues. If sometimes they disagreed with him, they felt that was healthy and natural. They saw their relationship with Wright as a stimulating partnership and a great improvement on the authoritarian tradition of many black churches. Rabbi Arnold Wolf of Hyde Park's KAM Isaiah Israel Congregation understood this, writing, "Many who call me their rabbi have taken political positions far from mine." He concluded, "A preacher speaks *to* the congregation, not *for* the congregation."

Wright did not speak for Obama. No two men could have been farther apart in important ways. Wright gloried in inflammatory rhetoric. Obama excelled at reticence. Wright did not advocate the armed overthrow of the U.S. government, but he was a harsh critic of its policies and of its allies, including Israel. Obama asked Americans to forgo bitterness in political disagreements. Wright's ego seemed to demand that he take the most extreme position and use the most startling language, as in his infamous "God Damn America" peroration. Obama is gratified when he successfully appeals to the broadest possible audience.

Obama did not look to Wright as a role model for his political career. He needed Wright's help in finding a way into Christianity that did not offend his intellectual standards while embracing his social justice concerns. Everyone who was pleased when Obama was elected president has to be grateful to Wright. Wright taught Obama how to talk about faith. Without that ability it is difficult to be elected president of the United States.

When it appeared that continued allegiance to Wright would jeopardize his presidential chances, Obama distanced himself from his pastor. Obama's exit from his church did not inspire others to leave. Hyde Parkers regretted the damage Wright's remarks did to Obama without rejecting Wright himself. Rabbi Wolf stirred up far more controversy within the neighborhood than Ayers, Wright, Jackson, and Farrakhan combined. His criticisms of the Israeli government's policies, especially its willingness to employ military force in Lebanon in 2005, and his support for a Palestinian state provoked real anger in Hyde Park and resignations from his synagogue. He did not grow milder as he aged. But he was valued by many of the people who disagreed with him because of his intelligence and his humor.

Of all these controversial figures, Rabbi Wolf was the only one actually useful to Obama during his 2008 presidential campaign. Perhaps the years of confronting angry members of his own congregation taught him to handle a hot topic. He consistently struck the right note. When Bill Ayers became an issue, Wolf dismissed him decisively as "a toothless ex-radical." Wolf wrote a highly favorable newspaper column about Obama as his neighbor (the KAM sanctuary is directly across the street from

KAM, the landmark synagogue across the street from the Obama home, confuses sightseers by its resemblance to a mosque, complete with minaret. (*City of Chicago, Dept. of Planning and Development*)

Obama's home), that circulated widely among Jews. He directly and effectively confronted the uproar over Reverend Wright and Jewish fears that Obama did not support Israel strongly enough.

When Wolf died in December 2008, Obama wrote affectionately of their disagreements: "He did it with kindness, and often with a smile or laugh to let you know that even though you were just plain wrong, and had no idea what you were talking about, he still loved you." Hundreds of Hyde Parkers recognized the accuracy of this portrait.

Finally, Hyde Park offers an incredible mix of political and cultural options to young people. I once judged a seventh-grade history fair project entitled "My Grandfather Elijah Muhammad." The student who prepared the project was a charming, intensely serious young girl of mixed race. Her carefully presented project included a neatly drawn family tree. I asked if she identified herself as a Muslim. "Not now," she replied thoughtfully, "but I am thinking about it, and my mother says that I can if I want to when I am older."

The sense that there are choices is the best part of living in Hyde Park. There may be easier places to live, but surely few that offer a young man or woman more encouragement to try something that may not have been done before.

TWO
A NEW KIND OF
COMMUNITY

A series of bold experiments conducted by determined people
made Hyde Park–Kenwood the unusual neighborhood it is. The
earliest of these experiments, beginning in the late 1840s, created
a new kind of community and provided it with remarkable cultural and recreational assets. This early experiment had nothing
to do with achieving a stable racial balance. But a hundred years
later, when the community did tackle race, its extraordinary assets were crucial to the creation of such a balance.

Paul Cornell, a young lawyer eager to make money in real
estate development, conducted the initial experiment. He arrived
in Chicago in 1847 at the age of twenty-five and soon bought all
the land that later became Hyde Park and several surrounding
communities. At this time the land was entirely undeveloped.

Cornell built the first homes and laid out ambitious plans for the future development of Hyde Park. The neighborhood, as he envisioned it, would begin eight miles south of downtown Chicago and border the lakefront. Hyde Park would be a self-contained, elegant enclave, benefiting from proximity to a growing city but sharing none of the liabilities of urban life.

Cornell was self-taught as a city planner, but he had at least one insight that proved he was a pioneer in urban design. In 1857 he traded some of his land to the Illinois Central Railroad to secure regular commuter service from Hyde Park to Chicago's downtown business district. Today his efforts would be considered "transit-based development." The coordination of planning for development and for the efficient use of mass transit is now essential for sustainable growth. His inspired pact with the railroad proved to be sound and original thinking and provided a lasting anchor for development in the community. The railroad, later electrified, still permits Hyde Parkers to commute without a car to the heart of the city in under fifteen minutes.

Cornell took other steps that made a major difference in Hyde Park's early development and still contribute greatly to the quality of life there. He banned heavy industry and worked for decades to secure a vast network of public parks. In 1869, before Hyde Park was annexed by the City of Chicago, Cornell and his supporters worked to establish the South Park system. It evolved into Jackson and Washington Parks, bordering Hyde Park. These extensive parks were planned by Frederick Law Olmsted and Calvert Vaux, the celebrated and successful landscape architects who also designed Central Park in New York City.

The breadth of Cornell's vision was matched by the efforts of the defenders of Chicago's lakefront, including Chicago's most famous planner, Daniel Burnham. These forward-looking activists, deeply resented in their day, kept the entire Chicago lakefront free of development. Hyde Park–Kenwood has easy

Paul Cornell, Hyde Park's founding father, left a thoughtful legacy, including parks and public transportation, for the community he loved. *(University of Chicago Library, Special Collections Research Center)*

access to the entire stretch of the lakefront, an astonishing recreational resource, thirty miles long from north to south.

Carefully cultivated natural beauty was retained as a permanent feature of urban living. (The motto "Urbs in Horto"—city in a garden—appears on Chicago's corporate seal.) This beauty is still valued. Thus the parks system has determined defenders today, including many Hyde Parkers. Unfortunately they often combine intense devotion with a narrow focus on preservation. They forget that the purpose of the parks was and remains that people may use them and benefit from the experience. As a result, benign improvements, such as adding paddle boats to an artificial lagoon, are fiercely resisted

Businessmen and professionals were happy to move their families to comfortable new homes in Hyde Park. Cornell led by example, building his own substantial home by the lakefront. He recruited family members as well. Hyde Park became a refuge for many of the white Protestant elite who were beginning to make large amounts of money in a rapidly growing city. To house them with appropriate style and comfort, the neighborhood now known as South Kenwood, adjacent to the north of Hyde Park, was laid out with oversized lots. Large mansions were built in a variety of styles on these lots, creating an elegant district. Today South Kenwood has pockets of seedy decay, but overall the neighborhood has aged gracefully. Pedestrians still slow their pace to enjoy the quiet and savor the rich architectural details that adorn the houses.

Cornell's ideas and investment paid off handsomely for him and for Hyde Park–Kenwood. His thoughtfulness about transportation and recreation are fondly remembered by current residents. Indeed, his photograph adorns the plaques given as annual awards to civic-minded citizens by the Hyde Park Historical Society. Illustrating the concern Cornell devoted to all the new community's needs, in 1854 he helped found Oak Woods Cemetery, just south of Hyde Park. Harold Washington, the first black mayor of Chicago, whose career inspired Obama, is one of many well-known Hyde Parkers laid to rest in Oak Woods. Fittingly for a diverse community, the cemetery today is owned and managed by blacks but includes a substantial Jewish section.

When in 1892 the City of Chicago decided to host a world's fair in honor of the four hundredth anniversary of Columbus's discovery of America, the lakefront and the parks made Hyde Park a desirable location. Daniel Burnham himself led the fair organizers on a tour of the parks. Rail transportation, introduced by Cornell, was expanded to bring visitors to the gates of the event. The fair was located in Jackson Park and on the Midway Plaisance, a green space that today bisects the University of Chicago campus.

Illinois Central trains arriving in Hyde Park for the 1893 World's Columbian Exposition. The IC trains remain useful and are beginning to look like the future of urban neighborhoods as the post-fossil-fuel-age dawns. *(University of Chicago Library, Special Collections Research Center)*

This fair, properly called the 1893 World's Columbian Exposition, was designed in large part by Daniel Burnham and Frederick Law Olmsted. It consisted of an elegant group of beaux–arts buildings, illuminated at night with dazzling new electric lights. The setting, on artificial lagoons in the huge park by the lakefront, was unequaled. The fair was a fantasy city, built of plaster and lath, largely on landfill. The venture was a huge success, attracting 27 million visitors, equaling approximately half the population of the United States at the time.

The fair symbolized high expectations for the future development of Chicago. The city was growing quickly and appeared to enjoy many natural advantages. Daniel Burnham ardently believed that careful shaping of the urban environment would create a new civic culture, benefiting all Chicagoans. The fair seemed a foretaste of that culture. But as the fair brought the world to Chicago, many observers noted that the city did not resemble the beautiful "White City" built for the fair.

At the fair, even vice looked attractive. "Little Egypt," the famous belly dancer who performed on the Midway, provided a thrilling, nonthreatening glimpse of the sexually exotic East. By contrast, W. T. Stead, a crusading British journalist who visited Chicago during the fair, provided a terrifying account of vice and corruption in Chicago in a book entitled *If Christ Came to Chicago.* Stead included a detailed map of the notorious First Ward, the most crime ridden section of the city, showing the location of brothels, saloons, and other iniquities, as the frontispiece of his book. His map presages the neighborhood maps of social scientists, with its effective use of color and careful delineation of activities. The rows of brothels glow in bright orange. The message was clear: sin dominates the center of what should be a Christian city and constitutes a dagger pointed at the heart of civic culture. Thus the fair became the basis for a stirring call to action, with consequences for the progressive politics that became important to many Hyde Parkers.

In Hyde Park the fair remains present today in improvements in the lakefront parks, including a decorative island ornamented with a Japanese garden. The fair's architecture remains in the huge, imposing, Greco-Roman temple that was once the fair's Palace of Fine Arts building and today houses the Museum of Science and Industry.

The history of the Palace of Fine Arts building is a fascinating example of the evolution of a community asset. It was intended to last for only two years as were all the fair's other impressive but temporary structures. Because it housed valuable art objects, the interior construction was of fireproof brick, though the outside was covered with temporary plaster and lath. Immediately after the fair, the Field Museum of Natural

The Court of Honor surrounding the lagoon at the Columbian Exposition. The "White City" dazzled fairgoers during its two years of existence. *(University of Chicago Library, Special Collections Research Center)*

History, then known as the Columbian Museum, opened in the Palace of Fine Arts. Many of the objects displayed had been exhibited at the fair. This new museum was a huge success and in 1921 moved to a larger home of its own in Grant Park, nearer Chicago's downtown. The Palace of Fine Arts deteriorated but was saved from demolition by a determined citizens' campaign. Competing proposals were advanced for the use of the building. Julius Rosenwald, the multimillionaire philanthropist who lived in Kenwood, tipped the scales in favor of a science and technology museum with a three-million-dollar donation. The exterior plaster and lath was replaced by limestone and the interior transformed to celebrate the wonders of science and industry, complete with a working coal mine shaft. The Museum of Science and Industry proved a national success. Until Barack Obama ran for president, mentioning the museum was the easiest way to identify the neighborhood, as far more people visited Hyde Park to tour the museum than for any other purpose.

If Hyde Park itself was the first experiment, and the fair the second, the third was a new university. The University of Chicago was founded there in 1890 with major financial support from the oil magnate John D. Rockefeller. In 1891 a brilliant young scholar of Greek and Hebrew, William Rainey Harper, was recruited to lead the new enterprise as president. Harper's vision of a university was a radical departure for American universities. It can be best understood as a new venture in higher education, bringing the rigor of a European research center to a new, rapidly changing city in the American Midwest.

Intriguingly, this radical vision was housed in very traditional buildings. Like the fair, the university was an architectural fantasy that left a defining impress on Hyde Park–Kenwood. The chosen style was Gothic and Tudor buildings, replete with gargoyles. Soon after the university's founding, ornate grey halls and abbeys began to rise in a cow pasture. The fantasy was backed by more than ample funding and notable determination. Carl W. Condit, a leading authority on Chicago architecture, observes that "the rate of expansion of the physical plant was probably unmatched in the history of American universities." By 1930 the campus consisted of sixty-seven buildings attractively laid out on two quadrangles. The style has suited the tastes and nourished the dreams of countless scholars. Its lack of modernity proved comforting and aided the university's later role as a haven for refugee academics in World War II. It served as a piece of faux Europe, which became a refuge as so much of the real Europe was pounded by bombs during the war.

Harper used Rockefeller's money to pay faculty about twice what they would earn elsewhere. But more was expected of them. Harper divided the full year into four quarters, underlining that each quarter, including the summer, should be used for

The Museum of Science and Industry, above, has recently been elbowed aside by the Obama home as Hyde Park's most famous tourist attraction. *(Museum of Science and Industry, Joe Ziolkowski)*

research or teaching. The faculty was also expected to increase productivity by teaching in the large extension program. And the university offered correspondence courses too.

The new University of Chicago soon developed a special orientation toward the study of the city. The first sociology department at an American university was established there in 1892. Albion Small, the founding chairman, was among the seven college presidents that Harper recruited to head academic departments. Small wrote nothing that is read today, but he built a tremendously influential department that shaped the teaching of sociology in colleges and universities across the country. He told his faculty and students that Chicago was their laboratory. The work of these early sociologists, later known as the Chicago School of sociology, included pioneering studies of the city as a growing and changing organism. The leading scholars of the Chicago School had no unified theory or doctrine. They wanted

A recent view of the Midway, which runs through the University of Chicago campus. Hyde Park's parks and green spaces are beloved and sacred. *(University of Chicago Library, Special Collections Research Center)*

sociology to be a science but disagreed profoundly about what that meant. Their disagreements, however, never undermined their self-confidence.

This increasingly diverse group of scholars immersed themselves in the processes of urban life. They conducted surveys and drew maps. Probably their most important contribution to civic life was not any specific insight or conclusion but their confidence in an expanding realm of social scientific knowledge. They believed that the city could and should be studied and that social change could be understood and eventually directed.

In addition to the new field of sociology, the university included a school devoted to the new profession of social work. Determined lobbying by Edith Abbott and Sophonisba Breckinridge, pioneers of research-based social work, propelled the School of Social Service Administration into the reluctant arms of the university in 1924. Through sheer force of will, the

William Rainey Harper, first president of the University of Chicago, sought to influence public and private education at every level. *(University of Chicago Library, Special Collections Research Center)*

two women prevailed over the objections of well-regarded and well-placed male opponents who preferred to be affiliated with charitable organizations rather than a university. Abbott and Breckinridge were two-thirds of a famous trio that included Abbott's sister Grace. They were loyal friends and highly productive scholars. Their work on child welfare, immigrant rights, labor, and race relations, among other subjects, shaped major government initiatives, including Social Security.

These women faced imposing obstacles—social, political, and academic—and each one experienced professional setbacks. But they made careers for themselves without female role models, partly at a major university and partly in the public sector.

Sociology and social work were new fields of study. But the university did not neglect more traditional academic disciplines. Harper was determined that the university would be a great center for the study of religion. He used the first $100,000 of Rockefeller's money to lure the Baptist Union Seminary, all that remained of the first ill-fated University of Chicago, to Hyde Park. The seminary became the university's divinity school. Other major Protestant seminaries subsequently located in Hyde Park, close to the University of Chicago campus. The ingathering continued long after Harper's death in 1906. In 1967 the Lutheran School of Theology moved to an impressive new building near the campus. And in 1968 the largest Catholic graduate school in America was launched when seven religious orders came together to build the Catholic Theological Union in Hyde Park.

Harper's ideas went well beyond amassing theological talent. He encouraged the study of religion along new lines by demanding the highest standards of scholarship, which in turn changed attitudes, particularly about non-Christian religions. The World's Parliament of Religions, held in Chicago in conjunction with the 1893 Columbian Exposition, was not organized on the basis of equality among religions as Christianity was clearly perceived as paramount. But representatives of Islam, Judaism, Buddhism, and Hinduism were listened to respectfully. In the same way new programs of study at the university, including the history of religion and comparative religion, encouraged scholars to understand a wide variety of religious experience.

During his presidency Harper also served as Sunday School superintendent for the Hyde Park Baptist Church. Both the Baptists and the broader American Christian community expected a lot from this new university led by a devout scholar. But the public was not always pleased with the work of the university faculty. The uproar greeting the 1906 publication of *The Finality of the Christian Religion* by George Burman Foster, a university professor, is a famous example. Foster argued that the "forms" in which Christian beliefs were expressed could and should change as knowledge increased, as long as the "substance" of faith remained the same. He was drawn to new ideas in philosophy and the arts, writing for example about Nietzsche and Ibsen. But he remained a fervently engaged evangelical Christian.

More conservative evangelicals, on the other hand, felt the "forms" of Christianity were as sacred as its "substance" and inseparable from each other. Foster's work disturbed them deeply, especially coming from someone who considered himself one of them in crucial ways. The Chicago Baptist Ministers Conference condemned Foster's book as "subversive of the vital and essential truths of the Christian faith." Demands were made for Foster's ouster from the Baptist community, but the Hyde Park Baptist Church stood by him. The dispute provoked by Foster's arguments remains at the center of current debates between modernizing and fundamentalist Christians.

The University of Chicago staunchly supported Foster's right to express his ideas. But there was already plenty of uproar within the scholarly community over the correct approach to the study of religion. Sociologists, historians, and anthropologists debated the issue. This controversy, never resolved and sometimes unpleasantly hostile, stimulated growing interest in other peoples' religious lives. While no method of study won out, and certainly none was free of cultural bias, an enormous shift occurred within the seminaries, from an approach limited by missionary goals to a greater respect for religious diversity.

By 1930 Jews had become the largest ethnic group in Hyde Park, but the Protestant churches and the seminaries remained popular and prestigious. Substantial numbers of Catholics also lived in Hyde Park. Inevitably the community became home to a lively mix of religiously inspired organizations, and gradually the social makeup of these organizations broadened. The first interfaith organization was founded in 1911 and by 1939 was known as the Hyde Park and Kenwood Council of Churches and Synagogues. As these institutions searched for common ground, the discussion often turned to social questions where it was easier to reach consensus than it was in matters of doctrine. This tradition of cooperation paid dividends when clergy from different faiths later helped the community face racial change.

Not every experiment launched in or near Hyde Park succeeded. In 1916 Frank Lloyd Wright designed the extravagant Midway Gardens, a combination of concert hall, ballroom, supper club, and public garden. Just five years earlier he had designed Robie House, a private home built in Hyde Park by a wealthy businessman. This groundbreaking building, once threatened with demolition, still stands in Hyde Park and attracts thousands of sightseers. The Gardens, an important social and cultural innovation as well as a pioneering piece of architecture, was built on the southern boundary of the neighborhood. By all accounts Midway Gardens was an extraordinarily successful fusion of high art and mass culture. Chicagoans were used to the tradition of the German beer garden, enlivened with music and dancing. Now they had a sophisticated version of the beer garden offering a venue for symphony orchestras and even Anna Pavlova, the famous Russian ballerina. Crowds flocked to the Gardens. Chicago's upper crust was delighted to dance or hold meetings there while the middle and working classes were also welcome to enjoy the entertainment. Unfortunately the enterprise was deeply in debt from the start and proved not financially viable. It failed and was demolished by new owners. Like the Columbian Exposition, Midway Gardens became a cherished, tantalizing memory. Ironically, unlike the fair, the Gardens were built to endure but left even fewer traces behind.

Life in Hyde Park was not all scholarship, religion, and good works. A wide range of businesses operated successfully. Taverns and cafés were numerous. At least two successive artists' colonies contributed to Hyde Park's slightly raffish reputation. The first revolved around Lorado Taft, the well-known sculptor. Suitably for a Hyde Parker, Taft was a formidable scholar, publishing important books on art history. He founded Midway Studios in Hyde Park in 1907 and trained many young artists there. His monumental Fountain of Time stands at the west end of the Midway Plaisance. His support for other artists included a progressive streak. Taft famously allowed women sculptors to work on the ornamentation of the 1893 World's Columbian Exposition, thus breaking a significant barrier.

Gertrude Abercrombie, a surrealist artist, who was a notable member of a later group of local artists, broke equally significant social barriers between black and white artists. Her work had the naive, very personal quality of a self taught artist.

Other artists of note were associated with Hyde Park, but Abercrombie had a special connection with the community. Although emotionally fragile and eventually overcome by alcoholism, she had a particularly strong presence in the neighborhood and in the lives of other artists. She literally took her art to the street and helped found the Fifty-seventh Street Art Fair, a fixture on the Hyde Park scene for more than fifty years. Her personal style is remembered even by Hyde Parkers who encountered her only at the art fair when they were children.

Abercrombie ran an eccentric salon for artists, musicians, and writers in her Hyde Park home. Her friends hailed her as the "Queen of Hyde Park." Her love of jazz brought black musicians, including Sarah Vaughan and Dizzy Gillespie, to the gatherings she organized. Her racially diverse parties presaged the interracial socializing that would come later.

Moving from interracial social contacts among artists and musicians to the community that welcomed the young Barack and Michelle Obama required a sea change. Over time white Hyde Parkers decided to share housing opportunities in their deeply valued neighborhood with black people on an equal basis. Reaching this decision demanded profound changes in the way white Hyde Parkers thought about race.

Hyde Park's rich institutional and social mix attracted creative people with new ideas that sometimes had far-reaching consequences. Hyde Park was still overwhelmingly white when radical theories about racial prejudice were developed by some major scholars connected with the University of Chicago. Today these conceptions are commonplace, even dull. That was not true when they were first conceived.

The purpose of the first American sociological treatises on race was to justify slavery. In the late nineteenth century the prevailing opinion in academic circles, as elsewhere, was that blacks were innately inferior. A crucial change in sociological thinking about race occurred in the work of W. I. Thomas.

In 1894 Thomas received the first Ph.D. in sociology granted by the University of Chicago. He immediately joined the department of which he was a founding member. He was committed to intellectual exploration and endless, obsessively detailed research. He found no evidence to support the idea of innate racial inferiority. In 1904 he wrote that racial prejudice was neither justified nor inevitable. He identified two types of racial hatred in America. In the South, where blacks and whites lived side by side, he spoke of a caste system developed to keep blacks in subservient roles. In the North he found whites motivated by a simple racial hatred, directed at a feared unknown. According to Thomas, both types of prejudice were irrational and could not be overcome by logical arguments. But rising above prejudice was possible if the conditions of life were changed to allow blacks and whites to interact differently. Prejudice, therefore, was not innate but the product of existing social conditions. At the outset of the twentieth century, this notion of prejudice as a transitory product of backward social conditions was as explosive as combining graphite and uranium.

In 1919 Thomas was forced to leave the University of Chicago because of a scandal in his personal life, but his influence remained. Robert Park, another founding member of the department, was committed to the objective study of race relations. In stark contrast to most contemporary academics, the early Chicago sociologists had all trained in different fields and pursued different professions. Park, who had been a journalist, had worked for Booker T. Washington, at that time the leader of the American black community, at Tuskegee Institute in Alabama. In fact he ghostwrote several of Washington's books. At the University of Chicago, Park considered himself a hard boiled realist, surrounded by "dammed do-gooders," sociologists who had trained for the ministry and were too sentimental to be good scientists. Despite his irascible demeanor, Park was invariably encouraging to black students in the department.

In 1912 Monroe Work, a black University of Chicago–trained sociologist, launched the *Negro Year Book: An Annual Encyclopedia of the Negro*, under the auspices of Booker T. Washington. Among many other facts, it provided an accurate record of lynchings, carefully analyzed by location and type, in an inexpensive format and readily available to the general public.

E. Franklin Frazier, a leading black intellectual who received his Ph.D. in sociology at the University of Chicago in 1931, was a fearless exponent of new thinking about race. In 1927 he published an essay examining the psychological reasons why white women falsely accused black men of rape. His willingness to share such ideas at that time literally put his life at risk. When Frazier was elected president of the American Sociological Association in 1948, he was the first American black to head a national professional association. His body of work was recognized throughout his profession, an indication that the new ways of thinking about race relations had become respectable.

This new departure emphasized the destructive consequences of the patterns of interaction between blacks and whites. Evidence of this destructiveness abounded. Violence was endemic in black-white relations. It is often forgotten how much racial violence occurred in the North as well as in the South.

One incident of racial violence brought a powerful response from Clarence Darrow, the celebrated criminal defense lawyer who lived in Hyde Park for many years. Darrow's reputation is inextricably linked with the sensational murder of fourteen-year-old Bobby Franks by Richard Loeb and Nathan Leopold, who like their victim were members of Kenwood's wealthy Jewish community. Darrow devoted his life to opposing the death penalty and broke new ground in using psychological insights to save Loeb and Leopold from hanging. This case and the equally sensational Scopes "Monkey" Trial, where Darrow defended a young teacher's right to teach evolution, have obscured his contributions in defending blacks against racially motivated criminal charges.

His most notable achievement in this regard was his closing argument in one of the trials arising out of the Ossian Sweet case. In a white neighborhood in Detroit, Michigan, eleven blacks were arrested trying to defend a black family from a white mob determined to drive them from their new home. During the altercation, a white man was shot and killed. In his address to an all-white jury, Darrow plainly declared, "I insist that there is nothing but prejudice in this case; that if it was reversed and eleven white men had shot and killed a black while protecting their homes and lives against a mob of blacks, nobody would have dreamed of having them indicted. They would have been given medals. . . ." These were remarkably honest words in 1925. Darrow's client was acquitted.

A substantial and determined attempt to change the patterns of interaction between blacks and whites in America was directed from Hyde Park in the first half of the twentieth century. Julius Rosenwald, the philanthropist, sponsored and guided this innovative and extensive effort. Rosenwald, of German-Jewish descent, moved to Kenwood after amassing enormous wealth as president of Sears, Roebuck. It is interesting to contrast his career with that of the better-remembered Henry Ford. Both men had keen intelligence and limited formal education. They were able, persistent, and extraordinarily successful in business. Both saw the opportunities presented by new technology. After making a great deal of money, both devoted much of their lives to philanthropic projects, including major innovative museums. Their institutions, Greenfield Village (Ford) and the Museum of Science and Industry (Rosenwald), still thrive and attract many visitors.

But as social thinkers their legacies could scarcely be more different. Ford is remembered as the man who fought the trade unions and hated Jews. He republished and circulated the Protocols of the Elders of Zion, an anti-Semitic forgery claiming to prove that the Jews seek world domination. Rosenwald is remembered primarily for his efforts on behalf of black Americans.

How did two such successful men come to look at major social issues so differently? There were temperamental differences. While Ford was suspicious and cold, Rosenwald was a genial optimist. When Rosenwald made a lot more money than he ever expected to have, he spent considerable amounts on his immediate family and on other relatives. After a while he thought his relatives had gotten enough, and he turned his attention to his workforce. In the 1910s and 1920s Sears was the Google of its day. Clever exploitation of new technology, including the rail network and the telegraph, allowed the company to offer its workers special perquisites, including a workplace environment considered luxurious at the time. Ford paid his workers well but spied on them until he was forced to stop by outraged public opinion.

Ford and Rosenwald moved in very different circles. Ford's closest associates were employees unlikely to challenge his thinking. Rosenwald, on the other hand, moved among equals, and as he became a philanthropist he acquired some impressive mentors. To begin with, he listened to his rabbi, Emil Hirsch. Hirsch was the spiritual leader of Sinai Temple, a Reform congregation in Hyde Park that attracted prosperous German Jews who wished to assimilate and participate fully in American society. Although sometimes derided as Judaism Lite, Reform teachings made major ethical demands on congregants.

Rabbi Hirsch preached a stern Judaism, stripped of the traditional practices he considered unnecessary. He valued the ethical teachings of the Torah above all else. He took as his role models the prophets of the Old Testament with their unwavering emphasis on righteousness and on confronting immoral authority. He told Rosenwald and the other millionaires in his flock that the poor had a right to a share of their wealth. Under Hirsch's guidance, Rosenwald supported innovative charities, for example the Family Finding Society, which tried to keep poor families together rather than send children to traditional orphanages.

If Rabbi Hirsch converted Rosenwald to philanthropy, Rosenwald discovered race relations on his own. Race relations were not a major topic in progressive circles in the first quarter of the twentieth century. Many progressives were focused elsewhere and had few expectations of improvement on this front; others were racist. Rosenwald was moved by reading Booker T. Washington's *Up from Slavery*. But the crucial influence was a biography of William H. Baldwin, the white railroad magnate who befriended Washington and raised money for his educational programs. Baldwin, Rosenwald wrote to his children, had led the kind of life he wished to lead.

Julius Rosenwald, the genial philanthropist whose imaginative giving kept his influence alive long after his death. *(University of Chicago Library, Special Collections Research Center)*

Rosenwald met Washington and visited the Tuskegee Institute. In turn, Rosenwald invited Washington to stay at his Kenwood mansion. Washington, the most famous black man in America, had been born a slave. His devoted mother helped him get an education after they received their freedom at the end of the Civil War. If Washington knew who his father was, he never revealed his name, and no man stepped forward to acknowledge him as his son. From these grim circumstances, Washington's rise was extraordinary. By the time he came to know Rosenwald, Washington was accustomed to advising rich and powerful white men.

Washington suggested to Rosenwald that he contribute to elementary schools for black children in the South. Washington was gratified by Rosenwald's willingness to be guided by his understanding of the needs of Southern blacks. He had received tremendous praise from white leaders but not much deference to his knowledge and insights.

Eventually Rosenwald contributed to the construction of more than five thousand public schools for black children in the South. The size and scope of that accomplishment is still impressive. Rosenwald, however, saw this work as just the beginning. He was convinced that helping black people lead better, fuller lives would change the way they were regarded by whites and therefore how members of the two races interacted. The key, he believed, was helping blacks develop their talents and achieve their potential as students, workers, and citizens. The breadth of this goal encouraged him to fund a wide range of projects. He supported black colleges and built black YMCAs. He gave money to the NAACP and the Urban League in their early years when these organizations especially needed support. Moreover Rosenwald turned out to be a gifted fund-raiser. He not only gave money but skillfully extracted money from other wealthy people.

To Rosenwald, racial prejudice was simply out of date and un-American. For America to advance, race relations had to change. Rosenwald's contribution was his hopeful and straightforward analysis of what he saw as the challenge, and his willingness to back his vision with his money.

Rosenwald remained a cheerleader on race relations even in the face of dreadful disappointment. He was delighted to visit American troops, both black and white, at the front in France in World War I. He urged white troops to offer black citizens "a square deal" and naively thought he caused no offense. He firmly believed the patriotic example set by black soldiers' bravery would win them new levels of acceptance in postwar America. Eventually and particularly after World War II, military service did play an important role in paving the way for blacks in American society. But the short term was far bleaker than Rosenwald predicted. For example, in 1919 thirty-eight Chicagoans were brutally murdered in the city's worst race riot, which began about two miles north of Hyde Park on an informally segregated beach. Even so, Rosenwald still clung to his belief that racial prejudice would wither.

Ten years after the race riots of 1919, the Michigan Boulevard Garden Apartments were opened just north of Hyde Park, in an overcrowded, booming, entirely black neighborhood called Bronzeville. Rosenwald financed the construction of this massive five-story apartment complex, which was always known locally as The Rosenwald. The development was designed to provide safe, decent housing for black families. The tenants were working people, not poor, and included professionals such as doctors and lawyers. The buildings were built as a business venture. Rosenwald hoped for a financial success that would inspire others to build similar developments. The return on his investment, however, was not high enough to attract other investors to similar projects.

But as a social initiative the buildings were enormously successful. The design provided quality housing and a host of amenities, including a Sears store and black-owned businesses on the ground floor. Child care was provided on site in nursery schools, one of which Rosenwald's daughter helped direct. The working- and middle-class tenants organized a multitude of cultural and educational activities for their families. Talented tenants, including Lorraine Hansberry, Gwendolyn Brooks, and Nat "King" Cole, added additional luster. In the late 1990s I asked an elderly black woman married to a postal worker how she and her husband had managed to send one child to Yale and one to Princeton. "Well," she replied, "I came up in The Rosenwald," indicating that her family had always aspired to a better life.

Rosenwald's reputation has probably suffered because of his association with Booker T. Washington. In the 1960s Washington fell from the extraordinary heights of public approval he had once enjoyed. Some of the criticism he received distorts the historical record. For example, Washington is accused of delaying the start of the civil rights movement by herding blacks into schools designed to dampen their ambitions. More likely, the civil rights movement was delayed by the concerted efforts of racist whites prepared to use every means available, including lynching, to keep black people in subjugation.

It is reassuring to modern ears to hear that W. E. B. DuBois, the militant black leader, honored Rosenwald as "the subtle stinging critic of our racial democracy." No one would consider accusing DuBois of delaying the civil rights movement. But when DuBois writes that Rosenwald's willingness to fund YMCAs for blacks was "a slap in the face of white Christianity," he is distorting Rosenwald's motives. Rosenwald paid for black YMCAs because he thought black people would benefit, not to expose the hypocrisy of white Christians.

Some people ask why the Rosenwald schools built in the South were not integrated. The answer is obvious: local whites would have responded with violence, and their actions would have been supported by local and state governments and unopposed by the federal government. Thus the children Rosenwald sought to serve would have suffered the consequences.

It is not absurd, though, to ask why the Rosenwald apartments were not built in Hyde Park. By the late 1940s the middle-class tenants of The Rosenwald would have been precisely the black Chicagoans that progressive Hyde Parkers hoped would choose to live in their newly integrated community. Why wasn't The Rosenwald built in Hyde Park or Kenwood in 1929? There are short answers. A large tract of vacant land was available in Bronzeville, lowering the cost of construction. Renting to blacks in any white neighborhood, including Hyde Park, at that time would have outraged white opinion, and black tenants might have faced mob violence.

But the question is really, how progressive were Rosenwald's social goals? The answer is that while he was far more progressive than most people of his time, his objective was decent housing, not integration. Rosenwald understood that influential white policymakers had to be convinced that blacks merited and could benefit from decent living conditions. Since no one else was both interested and willing to invest, he acted alone. His example was not followed.

Housing conditions in the "Black Belt," the overcrowded communities nearly all black Chicagoans lived in, continued to attract the attention of Hyde Parkers. In 1939 Jacob J. Weinstein, a deeply compassionate man known for his militant views on labor relations, became the rabbi of Kehilath Anshe Maarav (KAM), a Reform synagogue in Hyde Park. Weinstein encouraged his congregation to tackle difficult issues. KAM's social action committee studied the condition of black housing near their synagogue. Their thinking broke with the tradition of recommending improved housing within black neighborhoods. The committee recommended open-occupancy legislation. At the time it was a radical proposal.

The synagogue's own history provides an interesting sidelight on its determination to come to grips with the issue of decent housing for blacks. In 1924 KAM had moved to a new Greek Revival–style building in South Kenwood, which today houses the national headquarters of the Reverend Jesse Jackson's Operation PUSH. To move to Kenwood, KAM left behind a magnificent building designed by the noted architects Louis Sullivan and Dankmar Adler, a member of the congregation. The building, located north of Hyde Park, became the new home of the Pilgrim Baptist Church, a leading black congregation that was the fountainhead of the new gospel music. By the 1930s the building stood in the center of the lively, entirely black community of Bronzeville. When the building was constructed in 1891, the entire community was white. Thus synagogue members knew from their own migration how fast racial change occurred and what might have to be left behind when they moved.

World War II brought new energy to the discussion of race. During the war, the University of Chicago's Laboratory Schools, a private school serving children from nursery school to high school, were integrated at the insistence of the parents, not the administration. Marian Altschuler Despres, the wife of the independent alderman Leon Despres, and Fruma Gottschalk, another parent, wrote to the administration in support of the admission of black students to the Laboratory Schools. As Jews they specifically referred to the irony of opposing Hitler's Germany while maintaining segregation at home. They were successful in their lobbying, and generations of well-connected black students have attended the Lab School since. Their ranks have included Barack Obama's close advisers Valerie Jarrett, her daughter Laura, and John D. Rogers, Jr., and more recently Obama's daughters.

During the war another of Julius Rosenwald's initiatives helped the University of Chicago break new ground. In 1928 Rosenwald had established a foundation called the Rosenwald Fund. A strikingly modern feature of the fund was that all its resources had to be disbursed within twenty-five years of Rosenwald's death. One of the most interesting initiatives of the Rosenwald Fund was a fellowship program lasting from 1928 to 1948. During those years, fellowships were given to 587 blacks and 278 white Southerners for study and research in every scholarly field and the arts. The purpose of the fellowships was to support and celebrate black achievement. Whites who worked to create new opportunities for blacks also received assistance. It is difficult to name a famous black person from this period who did not receive a Rosenwald Fellowship. Marian Anderson studied music in Paris on a Rosenwald Fellowship while another helped Dr. Charles Drew, who pioneered blood banks, finish medical school. Zora Neale Hurston, Langston Hughes, James Baldwin, and Ralph Bunche all received support from the Rosenwald Fund.

In 1940 the painter Jacob Lawrence received $1,500 that proved to be one of the fund's most successful grants. He used the money to research and paint the Migration series, sixty panels depicting the movement of Southern blacks to Northern cities. The paintings were easy to understand and movingly conveyed the experience of hundreds of thousands of ordinary people. In 1941 they appeared in *Fortune* magazine. Their overtly didactic purpose, which would have gratified Rosenwald, did not limit their popularity or their status as fine art. The black community took enormous pride in Lawrence's work, art critics welcomed it, and people who had not thought about the Great Migration learned from it.

Edwin Embree, who administered the Rosenwald Fund, was assisted in his search for candidates by Charles S. Johnson, a young black University of Chicago–trained sociologist. Robert Park had drawn Rosenwald's attention to Johnson. With support from Rosenwald in 1921, Johnson published *The Negro in Chicago: A Study of Race Relations and a Race Riot*. Johnson studied race relations extensively and had a distinguished career at Fisk, eventually becoming its president. Johnson advised Embree not to fear controversy.

Edwin Embree hoped to underwrite appointments for black scholars at white universities by paying their salaries until the universities were convinced of their worth and would assume that responsibility. Black colleges did not offer sufficient opportunities for all the promising black academics and could not support their research on an appropriate scale. Although E. Franklin Frazier trained at the University of Chicago, he was not offered an appointment there, and neither Fisk nor Howard, where he taught, could fund the research he hoped to do.

Embree made an ambitious start to the placement of black scholars by persuading Robert Hutchins, president of the University of Chicago, to allow the Rosenwald Fund to pay Allison Davis's salary. Thus in 1942 Davis, an anthropologist, became the first black appointed to the faculty of a major research university. The Rosenwald Fund had previously supported Davis's research, but this appointment opened an entirely new door for him, transforming his career and paving the way for others.

Rosenwald died in 1929, and the foundation bearing his name ceased to exist in 1948. At first glance the social problems he tried to combat appear to have vanished, remaining only as distant, troubling memories. Today no one would ask for money to build schools for black children in the South. Black artists and scientists may apply for all sorts of public and private funding. Leading black scholars are fought over by prestigious universities. But because huge inequities in public education persist along racial lines, it is still worth looking at Rosenwald's work. He displayed a truly generous spirit on a very substantial scale and cooperated with the most talented among the people he sought to help.

After World War II ended in 1945, another wave of returning soldiers, black and white, began to arrive in Chicago. My father, Morris Janowitz, was among the former soldiers who used their GI Bill of Rights grants to attend graduate school at the University of Chicago. His doctoral dissertation in the sociology department analyzed how serving with black soldiers affected the attitudes of white soldiers toward blacks. His view that a personal sense of insecurity lay at the root of much racial prejudice attracted the interest of a refugee scholar, Bruno Bettelheim, who had had ample opportunity to reflect on the disastrous consequences of racial hatred during his imprisonment at Buchenwald.

Together they wrote the *Dynamics of Prejudice*, published in 1950 by the American Jewish Committee. The book focuses on lengthy interviews with one hundred Chicago veterans. Some remained rabidly anti-Semitic and deeply racist despite the achievements of both Jewish and black soldiers during the war. The book characterizes these individuals as failures who fear downward social mobility and who are also psychologically unhealthy, using hatred as an outlet for their anxieties. The book's message, reflecting postwar optimism, was that prejudice can be defeated by increasing prosperity, education, and an appropriate sense of self-worth. To Rosenwald, racists were unpatriotic; to Janowitz and Bettelheim, they were close cousins of the recently defeated fascists of Europe, a problem left over from the war, waiting to be solved. Their concerns echo Richard Wright's admonition regarding Chicago's South Side slums: "Remember, Hitler came out of such a slum." But they looked for fascism among whites, not blacks.

Sara Spurlark, who is black, arrived in Hyde Park in 1947 after attending graduate school at the University of Connecticut. In a sense she was following in the footsteps of her father who came to the University of Chicago in 1912 as a graduate student in mathematics. After a long and distinguished career in the Chicago Public Schools, she went to work for the University of Chicago's Center for Urban School Improvement. As Sara Spurlark recalls, integration was the goal of the idealistic young people in the community after World War II. She links this burst of idealism with the educational opportunities provided to ex-soldiers by the GI Bill. They wanted to live in a community that, in her words, "looked different from where they grew up."

THREE
A CRADLE OF
INDEPENDENT POLITICS

In 1889 when Hyde Park was annexed to Chicago, both the city and the community were profoundly changed. The addition was part of a huge acquisition amounting to 120 square miles of land lying to the north, south, and west of the existing city. Chicago doubled in size, becoming overnight the second most populous city in the nation and the largest in area. Hyde Park was transformed from a secluded, self-governing suburban enclave to a modest portion of a great city.

Before this, Hyde Parkers had been generally relieved not to be part of Chicago's rowdy, corrupt political scene. They were solidly Republican, and many had been strong supporters of Abraham Lincoln. The community was proud that Mary Todd

Lincoln and Robert Lincoln had lived for a time in Hyde Park after the assassination.

But by the 1880s Hyde Park's independent local government was proving inadequate in serving a growing, economically diverse population. The political elite, including the community's founding father, Paul Cornell, who remained active in local affairs through the 1880s, were committed to honest government but a very limited kind of government. The old guard was interested in protecting their property values. On different occasions they fiercely opposed brothels, taverns, and a turnpike. The major political accomplishment of Hyde Park's period of independent government was the acquisition of the huge and beautiful park system, which increased property values. This did not expand local government responsibilities because the new parks were administered by an independent, nonpartisan commission. Hyde Park's own government had only a few, part-time employees.

Newer residents were often interested in services that would require more village employees. Sometimes they were interested in services that wealthier residents did not need. For example, a proposal for a village library was defeated as many Hyde Parkers could afford the services of a private lending library. Newer residents challenged the old guard, but the government structure itself was inadequate. Simply because the older village form of government no longer worked, however, did not mean the only option was to join Chicago. A stronger independent government for Hyde Park was also discussed.

Annexation required a favorable vote from a majority of the population in those areas to be annexed. The campaign for annexation spurred widespread political organizing in Hyde Park, and the resulting debate deeply split the community. There were important questions to consider. Would Hyde

Park receive better police and fire protection? Would water and sewer service improve? And would the gains in services, if any, be offset by increased taxes?

The debate reflected the growth of Hyde Park's population and the area's increasing economic diversity. The crucial question of water supply is revealing. Hyde Park and Chicago both drew their drinking water from Lake Michigan. But Hyde Park offered an unequal level of service to residents depending on where they lived, because the location of its waterworks favored the wealthier north end of the community at the expense of the poorer south. Through annexation, residents of the southern portion of Hyde Park hoped to get more equal treatment. This disparity may have given the advocates of annexation the edge in the referendum because the poorer residents outnumbered the wealthier group and voted to join the city.

Temperance was another issue raised in the debate over annexation. Some residents, particularly those from the old guard, feared that urban ills would invade their community. The temperance movement aimed to prevent the social problems these Hyde Parkers feared. Temperance advocates were numerous in Chicago as well as in Hyde Park. In fact the Chicago City Council had passed a law allowing local districts to vote themselves dry. In theory it should have been as easy to achieve a dry neighborhood within the city as outside it. But it seems that at least some temperance advocates in Hyde Park felt it would be more effective to oppose liquor in a self-governing community than in a small corner of the city of Chicago. These residents felt autonomy would help them achieve what they considered a healthy community.

Annexation had major political consequences for both the city and the community. Hyde Parkers became directly involved in city politics. Hyde Park did not, however, blend into the larger political picture. Instead the neighborhood became

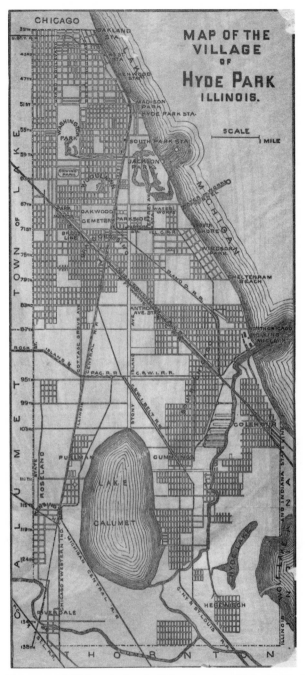

A pre-1889 map of Chicago's South Side, showing Hyde Park's location between Fifty-first and Fifty-ninth Streets along the lakefront. *(University of Chicago Library, Special Collections Research Center)*

a major wellspring of reform politics in Chicago, a role it has pursued to the present day. Rather than losing its identity by joining the city, Hyde Park became a unique urban neighborhood whose residents had a strong sense of being different from other Chicagoans. Hyde Parkers *were* different, in part because they had a different political agenda.

In the late nineteenth and early twentieth centuries the city grew at an incredible pace, the population increasing from 109,000 in 1860 to 2.2 million in 1910. After annexation, immigration continued to fuel growth. While many immigrants, especially blacks, came from within the United States, others came from abroad. In 1910, for example, almost 36 percent of all Chicagoans were foreign-born.

Ethnic loyalties dominated Chicago's politics. The city's leading politicians generally earned immigrants' support by dealing with the ward bosses who in turn controlled voting by distributing city jobs and other services. But the ethnic politics that dominated Chicago did not even register in Hyde Park. Few Hyde Parkers voted for the mayors who ran Chicago.

Annexation allowed Hyde Park to send two aldermen to the City Council. They were quick to criticize what they found in city government. Many Hyde Parkers remained committed to the style of politics that had served their community. They wanted to see justification for every tax dollar spent and were not interested in patronage. Hyde Park politicians particularly objected to the boodle system under which City Council ordinances were passed just to give a particular company a specific contract.

The Municipal Voters League, a reform watchdog organization, gave Hyde Park aldermen high marks for opposing boodle. In the early years of the twentieth century, two Hyde Park aldermen, William Mavor and Bernard Snow, managed to fight boodle and demonstrate leadership on the council. At different times each of them became chairman of the finance committee. This was a major accomplishment not equaled by a Hyde Park alderman again until 1983 when Harold Washington became both Chicago's first black mayor and the first mayor from Hyde Park.

Mavor also pushed for a public bathhouse and a building ordinance aimed at improving the city's terrible housing conditions. He opposed the transportation companies that overcharged Chicagoans and sought sweetheart deals. Mavor, Snow, and other Hyde Park aldermen stood up for their community's beliefs during council meetings disrupted by foul language and fistfights.

Hyde Park's boodle fighters contributed to the rise of a progressive agenda. The new University of Chicago advanced and broadened that agenda.

The founding of the university in 1892 and its subsequent rapid growth in both numbers and prestige brought together a talented group of people who disdained patronage politics. In addition to university faculty and students, 45 percent of the university's wealthy and well-connected trustees lived near the campus. Despite the university's Baptist affiliation, the trustees were a diverse group and included a number of Jews.

William Rainey Harper, the university's young president, and many of its leading scholars felt they possessed powerful new scientific knowledge capable of transforming urban life. They believed the results of their research into pressing social problems could shape effective remedies. The university community was eager to put their ideas into practice.

Harper accepted civic appointments, including membership on the city school board, in order to extend the university's influence in the city. He believed that strong partnerships with the business and professional elite would benefit both the university and the city. He did not fear the influence of wealthy businessmen because he assumed they would take direction from university experts. He encouraged faculty members to undertake projects on behalf of local service organizations. The trustees introduced faculty members to other local business and professional men who also supported their efforts.

The new university community included many educated women who were keen to participate in city government. To begin with, they wanted the right to vote. Some of the men supported this goal and others did not. Among the women were notable leaders willing to include working-class whites and blacks in their reform agendas, so that occasionally they got ahead of their male colleagues.

Important political players in Hyde Park also wanted to reform city government. Women wanted a voice, and men wanted to reorganize municipal government on scientific principles. People who are excluded from political power, or at least do not have the influence they feel they merit, frequently believe that the overall political structure should be reformed to grant them more access to power. Thus when Chicago annexed Hyde Park, the city's political leadership acquired, without realizing it, a vocal group of resident critics who eventually sought to displace them.

Over the years the membership of Hyde Park's political leadership changed to include Jews, women, and blacks. Regardless of race, religion, or gender, though, Hyde Park's political leadership remained well educated, self-confident, and critical.

Postannexation political activity in Hyde Park continued to center on the temperance movement. Temperance advocates saw alcohol as the vehicle that undermined communities with overcrowding, crime, and disease. Temperance advocates lost in Hyde Park, though they succeeded in keeping parts of Chicago and some nearby communities dry even after the repeal of national prohibition in 1933. It is easy but misleading to dismiss temperance advocates as petty cranks who unsuccessfully tried to run other people's lives. In fact the temperance movement tried to improve the lives of poor women and children. For example, the Women's Christian Temperance Union organized kindergartens and free clinics in Chicago.

The temperance movement was closely allied with the women's suffrage movement. In 1879 Frances Willard, an ardent suffrage and temperance advocate, became the first woman to address the Illinois State Senate. She spoke in support of the Hinds Amendment, which would have allowed women to vote on the issuance of new tavern licenses. Although she was allowed to speak only during a recess, a number of senators left the chamber in protest. In retrospect, the men who walked out of the Senate chamber were prescient since, as they feared, women's political activity would soon extend beyond temperance.

*

The "urbanization" of Hyde Park had begun before annexation. Excellent public transportation and improved roads brought the neighborhood closer to the city. South Kenwood, lying directly north of Hyde Park, remained an island of affluence, but other parts of the neighborhood included more middle-class and working-class people. As more apartment buildings were built and the retail sectors flourished, Hyde Park began to experience typical urban problems.

Residents, especially middle-class women, organized to provide new and better services to combat social ills. Many of these women had attended college and sought to take a professional approach to problems rather than rely on traditional, individualized charity. For example, the Hyde Park Neighborhood Club was founded in 1909 by local women to serve neglected and abandoned youth. The club emphasized the need for trained social workers to direct programs for young people.

Many of the same women also supported the work of Mary McDowell, a former temperance organizer turned union activist. In 1894 the University of Chicago appointed McDowell to run its Settlement House. This operation resembled Jane Addams's Hull House, which had opened five years earlier. The Settlement House brought educational, welfare, and health services to the desperately poor Back of the Yards community, located just northwest of Hyde Park. In sharp contrast to Hyde Park, where industry had been banned since the neighborhood's inception, Back of the Yards was home to the vast Union Stockyards as well as thousands of poor immigrant families. Conditions in Back of the Yards were appalling. Women who volunteered there encountered the results of insufficient health regulations very directly, in the form of huge, stinking, open garbage pits.

Mary McDowell later wrote of Evanston, the Chicago suburb where she lived as a young woman, "In Evanston, they knew all about temperance but very little about labor." Back of the Yards was the perfect place to learn about the lives of working people. McDowell learned that one in three of the babies born in Back of the Yards died before its third birthday. The residents' lives were wracked with preventable illnesses that often led to early death. She learned that habits of cleanliness and thrift, which temperance advocates prescribed as the path to working-class prosperity, were simply impossible to practice in the conditions created by unregulated industry.

The women influenced by McDowell were new to urban affairs and moved cautiously. They described their new concerns outside the home as an extension of the traditional feminine sphere. If women campaigned for new parks, for example, they tended to cast the issue in terms of how a properly administered park could strengthen family life. McDowell described her

Mary McDowell's long career embraced political activism, community organizing, social research, and administration. *(Library of Congress)*

work, including her ultimately successful campaign for effective, municipally owned and operated garbage collection, as "municipal housekeeping." But their objectives, however expressed, inevitably brought women reformers into conflict with the men who ran the city.

Mary McDowell, often described as the "Angel of the Stockyards," had some decidedly radical ideas. When unions were new and not widely accepted, she told a male audience that unionism "has done all these things for the men, but so far it has done nothing for the women. . . . They are receiving much lower wages than men get for doing the same work. The unions are leaving a loophole for their own undoing by not organizing the women, and the women are lowering their own position in the industrial world by not following the example of the men and forming their own unions." The question being fiercely debated at the time was, should unions be legal? McDowell accepted the need for unions in order to raise the standard of living among working people. She pushed past that controversial conclusion to demand that unions also serve women.

At the same time McDowell was committed to the research methods espoused by the new sociologists and social workers at the University of Chicago. She believed that further academic study of social issues would directly benefit poor people. She was equally prepared to use a study or support a strike to achieve her central goal of improving workers' standard of living.

For women who were struggling to enter political life, the first hurdle was obtaining the vote. In 1913 the Illinois state legislature granted women the right to vote in federal and municipal elections. In 1920 the passage of the Nineteenth Amendment to the Constitution gave women the right to vote in all elections. The long fight for suffrage taught women a great deal about organizing.

The national League of Women Voters was founded in Chicago immediately after suffrage was achieved. The decision to maintain a separate organization for women was controversial now that women could be full members of political parties, vote, and run for office. But many women felt they had a special nonpartisan role in voter education. Activist women belonged to the league and a host of other women's organizations bent on civic improvement.

Many people had thought giving women the right to vote would transform political life. Some believed women would elevate the moral tone of politics while others feared women voters might degrade democracy with their frivolous concerns. Neither happened. Women joined the parties men had built and participated in politics as they found it.

After passage of the Nineteenth Amendment, women in Hyde Park made progress that women elsewhere did not make.

This is partly because they were well educated and relatively affluent. Moreover Hyde Park's preoccupation with reform gave women an opening they would not otherwise have had. University of Chicago professors who aspired to political office welcomed the participation of women and needed their support. Women responded enthusiastically.

Many women favored Charles E. Merriam, one of the most famous crusading politicians to come out of Hyde Park. Merriam was a distinguished professor of political science at the University of Chicago who served on the City Council from 1909 to 1917. His decision to enter politics did not hinder his academic career or damage his scholarly reputation. His academic credentials helped convince Hyde Parkers that he was the reformer they wanted because he understood the value of their work. Naturally a community seeks a representative who is like them. Looking back on this period, it is fascinating to think that Hyde Parkers expected an entire, wildly diverse city to prefer Merriam to political types more familiar to voters. But they were not delusional, as Merriam grew to be highly popular in the city as a whole.

Hyde Park launched Merriam's career, but the issues he raised and the help he provided to all sorts of reform organizations attracted support from outside the neighborhood. He wrote, truthfully, that his office in city hall became the place for reformers to bring their ideas. Women who could not vote for him still flocked to his office because they received a positive response that transcended courtesy. He worked hard to share city and county government information with reformers who used it to promote their plans.

Merriam was a vocal advocate of allowing Chicago to determine its own fate by acquiring the independent legal status referred to as "home rule." Under Illinois law, home rule allows a municipality to determine the structure of its government and to enact regulatory legislation that includes different standards from those in effect elsewhere in the state. Reformers wanted home rule to increase the regulation of industry and provide new services. Businessmen wanted home rule to avoid interference in commerce and industry by the state legislature. Home rule was popular throughout Chicago and brought Merriam many supporters who may have been indifferent to social reform or good government concerns. After a 1904 amendment to the Illinois constitution, special state laws could be passed to meet Chicago's needs. But comprehensive home rule required the approval of voters across Illinois. Despite vigorous campaigns, home-rule proposals were defeated by statewide referendums in 1907 and 1927.

Merriam maintained "there is no more dramatic chapter in the history of modern democracy" than Chicago's struggle for home rule and honest government. Behind the rhetoric lies a deep and frustrated love of Chicago that is easy to understand. At a time when Chicago politics were dismissed as hopelessly corrupt, Merriam wrote defiantly of the need for "standards of justice, order, progress, appropriate to the dignity and power of one of the world's greatest cities." Chicago received full and clear home-rule status only under the 1970 Illinois constitution. Today, when Chicago's favorite son is president of the United States, the inability to control corruption at the city, county, or state level produces the same exasperated affection among Chicagoans.

The progressive message of the early twentieth century resonated particularly among women. They saw an enhanced role for themselves in Merriam's reformed city. On his part, Merriam noted in his memoirs that "women were less susceptible to the appeals of the machine than men, and on the whole responded somewhat more readily to the appeal of intelligence." Women entered progressive and later independent politics and provided

Charles E. Merriam, the quintessential professor/politician from Hyde Park, consolidated the community's early reputation as a hotbed of reformers. *(University of Chicago Library)*

important leadership in the cause. Part of the reason was purely practical. While the first black alderman was elected to the Chicago City Council in 1915, the first women (one black and one white) were not elected as aldermen until 1971. While both major political parties regularly chose black men as aldermanic candidates for black wards, neither party chose women as candidates for aldermanic seats except in a rare case as a "sacrifice" candidate. If women ran for the City Council, they ran as independents.

Interestingly Chicago is still waiting for its first Asian alderman. The most recent Asian candidate to come close was a woman, Naisy Dolar, running as an independent against a party stalwart. In 2007 she forced the party regular Bernard Stone into a runoff election but lost. Dolar received substantial support from Hyde Parkers. Despite the growing presence of Asians in Hyde Park, none has entered the local political arena.

In Hyde Park, where independent politics dominated, women did well. They ran campaigns and were elected to office, if not to the City Council. Merriam recognized the contribution Mary McDowell and other women made to city administration in fields not generally considered suited to women. He understood there was more room for participation by women in local than in national politics. He noted the strength and usefulness of women's nonpartisan organizations and how they helped shape local issues.

The political obstacles to progressive improvement Merriam discovered in the trenches of the City Council committee on gas, oil, and electric lights. His chief opponent in the battle for control of the development of city utilities was Samuel Insull. A close associate of Thomas Edison, Insull built the company that became General Electric. He also owned Chicago's major gas company and many railroads, including urban streetcar lines. Merriam described Insull as "intelligent, dynamic, realistic . . . this powerful figure stands astride the political straits of Chicago, entering into the reckoning and the plans of all who come that way." Insull understood that government regulators, controlled by the utility, could help build an unchallenged monopoly.

Insull's wealth gave him the power to corrupt government. "The Insull moneybags," Merriam observed, "became a center of political expectancy, his office became a center also of political intrigue and deals of far-reaching importance to the municipality, of quiet conversations from which impressive words went out as quietly through the community." These conversations determined what consumers would pay and what service they would receive. Merriam labored to have those conversations held in public where their real consequences for citizens could be accurately evaluated.

When Merriam and Insull fought in the City Council, the stakes were high. In the early twentieth century, the transportation, gas, and electric industries were booming in a rapidly growing city. Victory for the reformers was possible, because the City Council at that time controlled the city budget, approved mayoral appointments, and could create new city departments. Over time the council lost these enormous powers to a series of strong mayors. But when Merriam served in the council, aldermen could use city government power to control utilities on behalf of consumers.

In his memoirs, Merriam claimed that if Insull had acted with more integrity, he would have changed the course of Chicago history. Merriam saw Julius Rosenwald, not himself, as Insull's natural opponent. He considered himself a public servant who was unlocking the power of information and effective organization on behalf of Chicago's citizens.

Merriam had some notable achievement. He succeeded in establishing a commission to look at city expenditures. At one point he famously demonstrated that the city's own records contained proof that public money had been used to pay a firm for excavating shale rock from a tunnel actually filled with soft clay. But when Merriam's investigations became a real threat to corruption, his opponents on the council cut off the commission's funds. Rosenwald stepped in and paid to continue the investigative work.

Merriam thought that political science could be used to fight graft, corruption, and inefficiency. The roots of Chicago's problems, he believed, lay not just in immoral politicians but also in poor organization. Multiple units of government, with overlapping authority reducing efficiency, was as compelling a problem as a ward boss taking bribes. As a popular rallying point for reform, however, the ward boss was more useful.

Gradually Merriam became convinced that exposing corruption was not enough. His fellow aldermen did not act to protect consumers. Even when the costs of corruption were set before them, the voters did not reject venal aldermen. So Merriam decided he had to head city government in order to achieve real reform. In 1911 he ran for mayor as a Republican on a staunchly progressive platform. Republicans were often seen by progressive reformers of this period as a better alternative to the corrupt Democrats. Merriam led a well-organized progressive push to run the city as a smoothly functioning business machine serving citizens in new ways and without corruption.

In 1911 a professor in politics was not a target of mockery. Seth Low, president of Columbia University, had made a credible run for mayor of New York City during Merriam's time as a graduate student there. Woodrow Wilson, the former president of Princeton University, would soon be elected president of the United States. When Merriam ran for mayor, Wilson was serving as both governor of New Jersey and president of the American Political Science Association.

Low, Merriam, and Wilson all believed that scientific detachment benefited the study of politics and that the study of politics benefited the practice of politics. All three are linked to a specific progressive tradition that looked to corporate-style city managers to solve urban problems. Public outrage over the high cost of corruption and inefficiency gave progressives in this period the opportunity to test their theories.

Merriam's campaign in 1911 had many strengths. He was an effective campaigner. Like his incumbent Democratic opponent, Carter Harrison, he could address a crowd in German, a political asset in Chicago before World War I when 22 percent of the population identified themselves as of German ancestry. Jane Addams, whose reputation for good works was unrivaled in the city, endorsed Merriam. Julius Rosenwald, who rarely became directly involved in electoral politics, contributed $30,000 to Merriam's campaign and persuaded other wealthy men to contribute as well. Rosenwald also campaigned for Merriam in Jewish and black areas of the city. Harold Ickes, a brilliant, acerbic University of Chicago graduate, who went on to be one of the principal architects of President Franklin Roosevelt's New Deal, ran Merriam's campaign.

Merriam was extremely popular with the media of his day. The press loved his rhetoric and his exposés. Hyde Park politicians are good copy: they have a lot to say and they speak clearly and in full sentences. Reporters had liked earlier Hyde Park aldermen, but they had seemed to devote less time to the press and more to building working relationships with other aldermen. Merriam's success with the press and his relative isolation among his political colleagues echoes again and again in Hyde Park politics.

Merriam rose incredibly fast, from rookie alderman to mayoral contender, in a huge, growing city. Press adoration fueled his rise. There are eerie similarities to Obama's even more meteoric ascent. One difference is that Obama developed a strong working relationship with Emil Jones, the Illinois Senate president. Merriam never had that kind of relationship with a political mentor. Another major difference is that Obama's politics are inclusive across racial lines, and Merriam's were not.

On April 4, 1911, Merriam was narrowly defeated in the mayoral election. Ickes refused to reach out to mainstream aldermen and committeemen who were not progressive but who might have been willing to support Merriam, thereby contributing to his loss. Merriam believed he was the victim of vote fraud, which is likely but may not have been decisive. The black community voted overwhelmingly Republican during this period and therefore supported Merriam. This did not represent any sort of partnership between blacks and progressives. Merriam made no special overtures or promises to secure the black vote. In his memoirs, he dismissed existing black political leadership as hopelessly corrupt, though he expressed confidence that new, responsible leaders would arise. While Merriam analyzed individuals he admired such as Jane Addams, or loathed such as Samuel Insull, he did not mention a single black by name. He referred to Rosenwald as the best friend of Chicago's blacks, ignoring all local black leaders, among whom there were extraordinary men and women.

After Merriam lost the mayoral race, he continued to serve as Hyde Park's alderman until 1917. When the United States entered World War I he resigned as alderman in order to enlist in the army. He returned to Chicago after serving as High Commissioner for Information in Italy, eager to run for mayor again. He believed that his political appeal was enhanced by his wartime service, and that his chief opponent, William Hale Thompson, had been weakened by his isolationist opposition to the war. Women from both parties, including Jane Addams and Mary McDowell, rallied to Merriam's support. In language dear to his heart, Jane Addams said Merriam's victory would make "Chicago the pioneer in scientific administration of American cities." McDowell considered him the only candidate committed to real democracy.

Merriam underestimated the strength and audacity of Thompson's new political machine. He lost the Republican primary. His petition to be included on the ballot in the general election was thrown out by Thompson's allies. Nevertheless he received a substantial number of write-in votes.

Thompson proved more corrupt and arbitrary than his predecessors. In the eyes of progressives, he became the archvillain of city politics. A series of politicians controlled the city based on their ability to command large immigrant voting blocs. In deference to their efficiency, their political organizations were dubbed machines. Progressives chafed under machine dominance but never had a realistic chance to topple successive regimes.

Machine politics in Chicago gained national notoriety in the 1920s, linked in the public mind with Chicago's well-known gangsters. Ironically, victory in the fight for prohibition, a cherished aim of many progressives, only made the situation worse. Gangsters made enormous profits on illegal liquor sales and shared the proceeds with corrupt politicians.

Merriam had been an advocate of municipal suffrage for women when other progressive men opposed the measure. He expected women to be among the first to contribute to reforming politics and blacks to be the last. He looked for nobility in female politicians and found it. He looked for corruption in black politicians and found it.

Merriam finally acknowledged that reform organizations had failed to engage either working-class whites or political organizations based on ethnicity. He also recognized that women's organizations had a better track record of engaging their black, ethnic, and working-class sisters than male reformers did with their similar male counterparts.

Merriam did not, however, see a connection between the way progressives framed issues and their failure to reach immigrants or blacks. He was convinced that Chicago had a "Negro problem." In his eyes, blacks, the most recent immigrants, would be the hardest for Chicago to assimilate. Proof abounded in conditions in the Black Belt neighborhoods. In contrast, Mary McDowell rejected the Negro Problem. She wrote of Federal Street in the heart of the Black Belt: "Are these reeking alleys a Negro problem or are they a political problem? When Negro welfare is involved in bad housing, in child welfare, in unemployment, we are apt to call it a Negro problem instead of a human problem."

Not surprisingly, working for Merriam did more to boost the political futures of women than of blacks. Deeply disappointed when Merriam lost his second mayoral race, women continued to seek progressive candidates to support. For example, in 1923 four women ran for alderman in Chicago, all as independents—and all lost. The candidate from Hyde Park, Ella Walful, polled the highest vote.

Not all female candidates were unsuccessful. A prime example is Flora Cheney, a Hyde Parker who succeeded as a political organizer and as a candidate. In 1913 Cheney assisted her husband who served as Merriam's campaign chairman when he ran for reelection as alderman. This opportunity was her baptism into electoral politics. A natural organizer, her background included work around issues such as playground supervision and ensuring that children had access to suitable movies. Before her marriage to a doctor, she was a public school teacher and later served as president of the PTA at Ray elementary school. In 1920 she became the first president of the Illinois League of Women Voters.

Cheney's work for the league drew her attention to state politics. In both 1924 and 1926 she managed Hyde Parker Katherine Goode's successful campaigns for the Illinois House of Representatives. Cheney and Goode had been best friends for twenty-five years. When Goode died in 1928 while in office, Cheney ran successfully for her seat but died after serving only three months in the legislature. Both Cheney and Goode ran as Republicans, choosing the same party as Merriam for similar reasons.

Flora Cheney immersed herself for years in the issues that were and still are often considered "women's issues," including education, health, and recreation. But she was also intensely interested in reforming the state's fragmented voter registration system and rationalizing conflicting local election laws. After she died the legislature passed a law, dubbed the Cheney Bill in her memory, setting up a commission to study election laws throughout Illinois. Eventually her conception of a statewide system of voter registration was enacted.

Cheney's obituary, published in the *Hyde Park Herald*, praises her accomplishments in striking terms. Her talents were clearly valued by the community. In language that now sounds quaint, the *Herald* also noted the potential loss of female political leadership, referring to a "crisis in feminine politics." The *Herald* believed the community was used to having at least one woman among its representatives. The editorial marks real progress: including a woman among elected officials is not tolerated but prized.

*

The first generation of reformers from Hyde Park entered politics as progressives. They ran for office with the aim of making government more responsible, transparent, and accountable, themes that still resonate in Hyde Park today. Charles Merriam was the first professor from Hyde Park to seek elected office. His success as an alderman confirmed to Hyde Parkers the value of having an educated reformer, prepared to battle the city's leadership, as their representative. They continued to prefer such representation. Merriam's narrow loss in the 1911 mayoral election proved Hyde Park's preferences had drawing power outside the neighborhood.

The second generation of progressives from Hyde Park entered politics after 1930 and included two men whose political aspirations extended beyond the community. One of them, Robert Merriam, was literally the second generation as he was Charles Merriam's son. The other was Paul H. Douglas who, like Robert Merriam and his father, served as Hyde Park's alderman.

Douglas succeeded in moving from local politics to national politics as an elected official; Robert Merriam did not. One man's success and the other's failure would have been hard to predict as both were popular, intelligent, and able politicians. Both were also independent minded and thoroughgoing reformers. Both challenged the Democratic organization, an effective machine fueled by patronage. But Douglas had a gift that Robert Merriam lacked: he was able to reach working-class voters and persuade them that he shared their concerns. But that was not the only reason for Douglas's success. While Merriam's entire career was a direct challenge to the machine, Douglas moved up to national office with the machine's blessing, if not their earnest support.

Douglas taught economics at the University of Chicago. He is remembered today as the coinventor of the Cobb-Douglas function, still widely used in economic models to determine the relative contributions of labor and capital. Having grown up in extreme rural poverty, Douglas devoted his academic life to the study of how economic systems shape the lives of working people.

As a graduate student living in New York City, he worked organizing shop girls into a union. He was once arrested on a charge of blocking traffic while speaking outside a department store to a group of six people. In court he was appalled when the arresting officer lied under oath, stating that Douglas was addressing a large crowd and had shoved the police while swearing. He was found guilty despite his testimony and that of the people who were with him. The experience, he wrote, taught him to "understand the feeling of workers that the law and indeed the government were hostile to them." The empathy he acquired during that incident and while looking for work was key to his later success in political life.

Meanwhile he received his Ph.D. in economics from Columbia University. He was deeply interested in questions that we still struggle with today. For example, how should the minimum wage be determined? Should employees as well as employers contribute to the cost of unemployment insurance? He accepted capitalism and rejected the inevitability of the class struggle but advocated a far more comprehensive social safety net than President Franklin Roosevelt's New Deal ever envisioned. In his memoirs he describes "the flood of happiness" he experienced when early in his career he thought of supplementing the minimum wage with allowances for wage earners with children.

Douglas always ran for office as a Democrat, but he would have been far more at home in the British Labour party or among the German Social Democrats. He waited throughout his career for the formation of a new party where he would be more comfortable, but that never materialized.

Many Hyde Parkers share Douglas's discomfort. Obama's personal physician of many years, Dr. David Scheiner, views health insurance in ways that exemplify Douglas's thinking on social policy questions. Scheiner is an excellent physician who practices medicine in a utilitarian suite of offices above a couple of diners on Fifty-third Street, the closest thing Hyde Park has to a main drag. He lives near his office and makes house calls. Scheiner cannot understand why his former patient, whom he deeply respects, does not simply propose single-payer health insurance. Scheiner cites the excellent care his own son receives from the British National Health Service as well as a host of studies. He dismisses the idea that health insurance companies provide free or even adequate choice. "Whenever I see a patient," he says, "the insurance company is in the room with me."

Obama is too pragmatic to follow Scheiner's advice. But it is possible to see an echo of Douglas's attitude in Obama's distaste for partisan politics. Both men retain a vision of sensible people getting together to review policy options and making sound choices—a process that is hard to implement in this country.

In 1919 Douglas moved to Chicago and began teaching at the University of Chicago, an institution he cheerfully recalled in later years as being the same age as himself. He became involved in the same struggle against Samuel Insull and the exploitation of consumers by utility and transportation companies that had engaged Charles Merriam. Douglas described Insull at the beginning of their battle as "the uncrowned king of Chicago and of Illinois." Insull had sufficient political influence in the City Council, the state legislature, and the U.S. Senate to guarantee incredible profits for the utility companies he controlled. He made sure that politicians did not challenge the price he charged consumers. Insull used these profits to fund other riskier business ventures.

When the city decided to take over public transportation, Insull sought public compensation for his transportation companies (known at the time as "traction companies") that far exceeded their value. Like Charles Merriam, Douglas emphasized the political power of accurate information. When he examined the transportation companies' records, he recalled, "we actually found horses itemized that had departed this life many decades before, together with tracks and cars that had long since disappeared." To resist Insull's demands, Douglas joined with the elder Merriam and Harold Ickes to form the People's Traction League.

"It was a baptism of fire," Douglas wrote years later after a lifetime of battles. Insull counterattacked on all fronts and attempted to force the University of Chicago to fire Douglas. The professor was always grateful for the university's firm defense of his right to academic freedom.

Reformers were unable to stop Insull in any legislative body, but he was ultimately destroyed by the imploding markets of the late 1920s. Nevertheless Douglas's campaign to free consumers from the burden of supporting Insull's companies brought him national attention and the opportunity to write a reform law protecting consumers in Illinois. Douglas's political work was extremely time-consuming but never distracted him from academic research and publishing. What he learned in his political life motivated him to an impressive record of new publications.

Douglas got his start in local politics doing precinct work for Flora Cheney, who built an excellent field organization for the campaigns she ran. Cheney put Douglas to work on behalf of Katherine Goode and herself, who were both elected to the state legislature. Douglas learned precinct work. He was also convinced by the women's examples that idealistic politicians could succeed within a major party and make a real contribution. His view of Goode and Cheney, whom he described as "noble," guided his later decision to enter mainstream politics.

Douglas's use of words like "noble" as well as his comment that after spending time with Jane Addams he "felt strengthened, even purified" sound odd, even disturbing to modern ears. Contemporary women resist the pedestal Douglas seems to want to put them on, fearing they will be relegated to the sidelines. Douglas lived through a great transition. Women like Jane Addams and Mary McDowell were hailed as secular saints by observers like Charles Merriam. But when Douglas, seventeen years younger than Merriam, entered politics, women were not only voting but held elective office.

In 1935 Maynard Krueger, a University of Chicago economics professor, ran for Fifth Ward alderman, hoping to represent Hyde Park as a Socialist. Krueger, a Marxist, belonged to the "militant" faction of the Socialist party. Douglas had been sympathetic to the Socialists and had voted Socialist himself. Like Krueger, he wanted stronger government intervention on behalf of the poor than most Democrats would support. Their paths had diverged, however. Krueger worked to push the Socialists to the left. Douglas instead served as a campaign manager for Joseph Artman, a divinity professor from the University of Chicago who also ran unsuccessfully for Fifth Ward alderman in 1935. Artman ran as an independent Democrat and outpolled Krueger.

When Norman Thomas ran for president on the Socialist ticket in 1940, Krueger was his running mate. By then Douglas was in the Democratic camp. When he successfully ran for alderman in 1939 he accepted support from the regular Democratic party, proving that although he was an idealist he could make a pragmatic decision.

Right-wing commentators often characterize Hyde Park as a nest of socialists. They love finding out that well-known Hyde Parkers have said something positive about a socialist or even a Communist, or attended a dinner honoring Eugene Debs. Obviously there have been socialists in Hyde Park, and there are certainly a few even today. But these commentators go on to argue that somehow Obama's success is explained by his unholy alliance with socialists. The flaw in the argument is that the socialists in Hyde Park never won an election, not now or in the past. An alliance with Hyde Park's socialists might or might not be unholy, but it would certainly be unhelpful.

Hyde Parkers traditionally express admiration for socialists who are usually dead or foreign. Growing up in Hyde Park I learned the words to folk songs from the Spanish Civil War in three languages. But like most Hyde Parkers, I am a dyed-in-the-wool Democrat.

That does not mean that Hyde Parkers fit easily into the Democratic party in Chicago. Although Douglas received support from the party, like Charles Merriam he was very much the odd man out on the City Council. Like Merriam too, he often heard the term "professor" employed as an insult. Paddy Bauler, a fellow alderman, to whom the famous "Chicago ain't ready for reform" quote is attributed, frequently threatened to have

A study in contrasts: Richard J. Daley, left, and Paul H. Douglas shared few political goals but helped each other hold power in their respective spheres. *(Time & Life Pictures/Getty Images)*

Douglas beaten up or slipped a Mickey Finn. Over time some of his colleagues came to like him personally, but few ever voted with him. Douglas admitted that almost none of his colleagues on the City Council had gone to college, but he suggested that "in terms of innate intelligence most of them would have held their own with my colleagues on the Midway. I liked them and believed them to be better persons than most of the well-educated and wealthy utility lawyers who, living in the suburbs, looked down on those they helped to corrupt in the slum areas."

In 1915 Douglas had married Dorothy Wolff, a brilliant student who became an academic. They had four children. His wife shared his interest in progressive politics but, in her case, it led to membership in the Communist party. Douglas was distressed when they grew apart and divorced. But Dorothy's political views, particularly her status as a party member, would surely have hindered Douglas's later political career.

Douglas found his true partner in his second wife, Emily Taft, a Hyde Parker who was the daughter of the great sculptor Lorado Taft. He married her in 1931. She had attended the Laboratory Schools and the University of Chicago. Emily Taft was an actress who enjoyed a run on Broadway in the mystery play *The Cat and the Canary.*

Douglas shared her interest in the arts. In 1939, just after his election as alderman, he founded the Hyde Park Arts Center in an abandoned saloon, next to his newly acquired aldermanic office. Douglas was only one of a number of Hyde Park politicians to have an interest in the arts and in some cases a taste for the avant-garde.

The Douglases both searched for a religious community that shared their social justice concerns. Paul found that community in the Quakers; Emily found it in the Unitarian Church and occupied a number of important positions within the denomination. In an admiring essay on Thomas Jefferson, she wrote of the desirability of accepting differences in people's religious beliefs as readily as accepting their physical differences.

Her tolerance, however, did not extend to fascism. During a visit to Italy in the early 1930s, both husband and wife were deeply impressed with the fascist threat. They were fervent anti-isolationists. Both were convinced that the United States had to intervene militarily against Germany and Italy.

When World War II began, Douglas was eager to serve his country. At the age of fifty, and despite his tenured position and his years of Quaker involvement, Douglas insisted on enlisting in the Marine Corps. He was the oldest private ever to enter the service. He demanded combat duty, won two Purple Hearts and a Bronze Star, and lost the use of his left arm on the battlefield in the Pacific. It was a dramatic demonstration of the Hyde Park philosophy that you always have choices.

Meanwhile Emily Taft Douglas fought for their views on foreign policy on the home front. She served as chairman of the Illinois League of Woman Voters' section on foreign policy and worked for the International Relations Center in Chicago. In 1944, while Douglas served in the Marines, she ran for Illinois representative at large against Stephen A. Day, a committed isolationist who had opposed Roosevelt's foreign policy. She won despite a rabid campaign against her by the *Chicago Tribune*.

In the House, Emily Taft Douglas served on the Foreign Affairs Committee. She supported the work of the United Nations Relief and Rehabilitation Administration by helping to pass legislation funding the organization. In August 1945 she observed their efforts in Europe. She cosponsored legislation to put the United Nations in charge of the abolition of nuclear weapons and of arms control.

On the domestic front she voted against the establishment of a standing House Un-American Activities Committee (HUAC). She did not neglect traditional women's issues, conducting a successful campaign to fund rural bookmobiles. Officially elected to represent all of Illinois, Emily Taft Douglas stood up for prevailing sentiments in Hyde Park on issues like opposing HUAC and promoting libraries. After one term she lost her seat in 1946, in part due to her opposition to "bringing the boys home" immediately. She was concerned that too rapid a withdrawal of American troops from Europe and the Pacific would jeopardize international security.

In 1948 Jacob Arvey, a powerful Democratic boss, offered to support Paul Douglas for the Democratic nomination for the United States Senate. Douglas had served with Arvey on the City Council, where they often disagreed. But Douglas considered Arvey the ablest man on the council.

While Arvey wanted to make life difficult for the Republican candidate, he did not believe Douglas could win. Many observers at the time and since have felt that Arvey's motivation was to distract Douglas from Chicago politics because he would have been a formidable candidate for mayor.

Douglas had no money; few people thought he had any chance to win the general election. But he undertook a grueling statewide tour in a Jeep with a loudspeaker. He believed his wife's second campaign for the House of Representatives had been badly mishandled by state party managers. She had toured statewide but had met numerous county officials and very few voters. Douglas sought out any opportunity to meet ordinary voters. He stood outside factories as the night shift let out—before this became a clichéd photo opportunity.

To everyone's surprise, including his own, Douglas won. In his campaign for the Senate, he demonstrated that he possessed strengths as a politician that Charles Merriam lacked.

Like Merriam, Douglas was committed to progressive goals for city government, including transparency and efficiency. He picked up the progressive torch that Merriam had laid down, particularly in his struggle with Insull on behalf of consumers. But through his involvement with the labor movement Douglas had acquired a deeper understanding of the challenges facing working people. That work and his own early experience of deprivation allowed him to connect deeply with ordinary people whose position in life seemed very different from that of a university professor.

After Douglas became a senator he relied heavily on his wife's tact and political instincts to balance his impatience with the social requirements of political life in Washington. Douglas wrote of her: "Emily combines idealism with a woman's sense of caution, and integrity with a politician's sense of timing, qualities that have saved me from many mistakes." While Paul and Emily Taft Douglas can be seen as a "power couple" similar to the Clintons or the Obamas, Mrs. Douglas had far more political experience in her own right when her husband entered the Senate than Ms. Clinton or Mrs. Obama had when they reached the White House. In few couples have both individuals held national office—still fewer where the wife has achieved national office before the husband. Douglas wrote, "It would have been only human if Emily had resented the way I replaced her in the political arena," but he insisted he never saw any sign of envy.

After her career in office ended, Emily Taft Douglas took up writing, publishing a successful children's book; a biography of Margaret Sanger, the pioneering advocate for birth control; and a study of women whose careers opened new opportunities for other women.

In his first term Paul Douglas achieved a remarkable status in the Senate. In 1952 he was widely mentioned as a possible presidential candidate, in part because of his enormous popularity with the Washington press corps. He was a stellar example of the media's preference for Hyde Park politicians.

Douglas was known particularly for his commitment to civil rights, consumer rights, and public housing. On civil rights issues he was almost as alone in the Senate as he had been in the City Council. At the same time he was a notable cold warrior, supporting the Korean War, the refusal to recognize Communist China, and the expansion of the military.

Douglas tangled with Senator Joseph McCarthy only indirectly. He spoke out against the misuse of congressional committees, offering "ten commandments" to ensure fair play in all committees. McCarthy, of course, had broken all ten strictures. Although his liberal credentials were second to none, Douglas was reluctant to attack McCarthy directly for two reasons. First, on principle he disdained personal attacks. Second, he was convinced that communism was a terrible threat to democracy and had no patience with fellow travelers.

In 1954 Douglas faced a bruising campaign for reelection. His opponent, Joseph T. Meeks, a Republican businessman and lobbyist, was as relentless a campaigner as Douglas and willing to aim low. Meeks attacked Douglas as the "Senior Socialist Senator" from Illinois. Meeks attempted to smear Douglas with corruption charges allegedly arising from a Federal Housing Authority loan to a Chicago developer. But Homer Capehart, the Republican chairman of the Senate Banking Committee, pointed out Meeks's errors and cleared Douglas's name. Capehart's action reflected the reputation for integrity that Douglas had earned on both sides of the aisle. Meeks also attempted to play the McCarthy card, closely associating himself with the Wisconsin senator.

The *Chicago Tribune* struggled with Douglas's record, just as modern right-wing bloggers struggle to build up their Hyde Park socialists for an Obama conspiracy. Douglas would have been easy to smear on the basis of his progressive politics and earlier support for the Socialist party—if not for his impeccable record as a cold warrior. So the newspaper grudgingly acknowledged his anti-Communist credentials and spearheaded a vicious statewide campaign against him anyway.

Douglas won decisively. A major factor in his victory was the massive support he received from the Cook County Democratic Organization and the Chicago machine. Battered by a series of scandals, the machine wanted the association with a candidate of Douglas's caliber. His standing in Washington would help Chicago, and he would not be able to interfere much in local affairs. The machine's warm embrace of Douglas in 1954 reminds an observer of Mayor Richard M. Daley's heartfelt attachment to Barack Obama, for similar reasons.

In the Senate Douglas continued to champion civil rights. Martin Luther King hailed him as the best of senators. He fervently supported Hubert Humphrey's efforts to open up the national Democratic party to blacks. Emily Taft Douglas marched with King at Selma. Douglas was proud of her and supported her in every way he could. She was far from being the only Hyde Parker on the march.

Meanwhile Douglas was also a notable advocate for the environment. He launched a successful campaign to save the Indiana Dunes, which he had long considered a prime example of nature as "an ever-present source of physical and spiritual renewal." Hyde Parkers remember Douglas's work to preserve the Dunes perhaps better than any other of his achievements, because they see the creation and preservation of parks as a crucial ongoing battle.

In 1966 Douglas was defeated by the Republican Charles Percy. Percy was far younger than Douglas, who was now seventy-four. His cold war attitudes had begun to seem dated. Percy's daughter was murdered during the campaign, which created a wave of sympathy for him.

Percy was also able to skillfully exploit fears created by Douglas's strong support for open housing. In his memoirs Douglas carefully notes that Percy lived in Kenilworth, a Chicago suburb that had effectively excluded both Jews and blacks. Douglas pointedly records his pride in Hyde Park as a successful integrated community.

*

After Douglas resigned as Fifth Ward alderman in 1942, no major political figure held that position until 1948 when Charles Merriam's son Robert was elected. Robert Merriam was a wonderfully appealing, new incarnation of the old progressive tradition his father had once exemplified. He was young, good-looking, and articulate. Television would have loved him and would have helped his career had it been available to him. Moreover he was a war hero who had fought through the Battle of the Bulge and then written a book describing it.

In some ways Merriam and Douglas brought similar strengths to the political arena. Both were smart and well educated but could rely on their military service to avoid being labeled elitist. Both were pragmatic. Douglas accepted support from the regular Democratic party. Merriam agreed to run for mayor as a Republican, though he was a Democrat.

This happened in 1955 when Richard J. Daley first ran for mayor and the Republicans recruited Merriam to run against him. The issue for Merriam and his supporters was not whether or not they were Democrats. His Hyde Park supporters were Democrats and remained Democrats at every other level of government. The issue was the opportunity to challenge the Cook County Democratic Organization as machine politicians, not as Democrats. Douglas had sidestepped this issue by moving to Washington. But anyone who aspired to be mayor of Chicago had to confront it head-on.

In retrospect the 1955 election may look like the founding of a dynasty because Daley remained in office until 1976, and his son is mayor today. But Daley's victory was far from inevitable at the time. Merriam hoped to assemble a coalition of

Robert Merriam's career as Hyde Park's leading reform politician never fulfilled its early promise. *(University of Chicago Library, Special Collections Research Center)*

reform-minded voters from both parties. He went outside the party in his efforts to defeat the machine. He hoped to free the Democratic party in Chicago to become an open and accountable organization. Indeed, Merriam might have rejoined the Democratic party if he had won.

Merriam wanted clean government that was also creative and willing to tackle people's problems. For example, he proposed a system of passenger transfers between the city's elevated electric trains and buses, which Chicagoans found highly useful when it was finally implemented decades later.

Merriam's defeat by Daley in 1955 was as much a watershed in that generation of progressive politics as his father's defeat had been in 1911. Afterward Hyde Parkers who wanted to be

Democrats at every level of government either had to accept machine politicians in local offices or support so-called independent Democrats who refused to join the machine.

Many explanations have been offered for Merriam's loss to Daley. They include vote fraud, the strength of Daley's political organization, Daley's allies' skillful defaming of Merriam among Catholic voters as the husband of a divorced woman, and allegations that Merriam was too well educated and urbane to relate to ordinary working people. All these factors probably contributed to Daley's victory.

But the element in Robert Merriam's defeat that is most interesting in view of Hyde Park's later political history was his failure to ignite enthusiasm among black voters. The black vote went solidly to Daley. The *Defender*, Chicago's leading black newspaper, editorialized on behalf of Daley in terms that would startle anyone familiar with his later record on race relations. It appears that the reformers still saw the black community primarily as a social problem to be solved, not an ally in the fight for reform.

After the younger Merriam's defeat, no reformer had a real chance at winning a mayoral election until Richard J. Daley's death in office in 1976. Frustration with repeated defeats encouraged political reformers to concentrate not on challenging Daley in the polls. Instead they turned to lawsuits in seeking to curb his power through the courts.

*

Well-educated and thoughtful politicians from Hyde Park enjoyed unequal success, reflecting the obstacles in their path and their different abilities. Paul Douglas could communicate effectively with working people. Ordinary voters across Illinois saw him as a powerful spokesman on their behalf, not a distant professor. That ability propelled him to the U.S. Senate. His own moral insights also compelled him to speak out for the black community. In contrast, Robert Merriam's talents never took him beyond his City Council seat, in part because he could not make that kind of connection with working-class voters or inspire black voters.

It is interesting to speculate about Chicago's history if Douglas had ignored Arvey's offer of support for the Senate nomination in 1948. He might have, as it was not a very good offer—it included no money or active support. If Douglas had plunged back into Chicago politics and run for mayor, he might have won. His ability to reach working-class voters and his willingness to put civil rights on the front burner might well have earned him supporters that Robert Merriam could not attract. It is tantalizing to imagine what Chicago would have been like under a mayor committed to civil rights and reform. Hubert Humphrey, whom Douglas deeply admired, was such a mayor after being elected in Minneapolis in 1945.

The first generation of reformers from Hyde Park focused on Washington, D.C., when they were unable to take control of city government. Their influence can be seen in many New Deal programs, including Social Security. The second generation of reformers followed a similar path. Douglas won far more votes in the U.S. Senate than he ever won in the City Council. After his career in city politics ended, Robert Merriam went to work on President Eisenhower's staff. The work of transforming the Chicago City Council into a legislative body and undertaking political reform still needed to be done.

The question of who would lead Chicago's next push toward reform remained open. The first and second generations of reform politicians from Hyde Park were white. In the 1960s reform-minded Hyde Parkers began to understand the pressing need for strong and effective black leadership, and not only for the sake of improving life for the black community. The civil rights movement demonstrated that black leaders could make America a better place as well as help their own community. The demographics and political history of the South Side of Chicago indicated that Hyde Parkers had an increasing number of opportunities to support talented black politicians.

Reformers had raised the banner of good government in the state capitol in Springfield, and in the U.S. Congress. But no reform candidate for mayor from Hyde Park had triumphed at the polls until Harold Washington, Chicago's first black mayor, won in 1983. That election marked the convergence of black politics and reform.

FOUR
EARLY BLACK POLITICS

The first blacks to enter Chicago politics did not do so from
Hyde Park because they could not live there. Successful early
black politicians rose to power representing the neighborhoods
created by the migration of blacks from the South to Chicago
in the early twentieth century. The wealth of black talent in
Chicago reflected the city's drawing power in this period and
the continuous "brain drain" of ambitious young people from
South to North.

The *Defender*, Chicago's leading black newspaper, was
founded in 1905. Its purpose was not just to defend the interests of black people in the political arena but to defend them
literally—by protecting them from extralegal physical violence.
In the 1910s the *Defender*'s editor, Robert S. Abbott, conducted

a famous campaign urging Southern blacks to move to Northern cities. Many people responded to his call, and some found opportunities for advancement in the North that they would not have had in the South. Between 1900 and 1944 the black population of Chicago grew from 30,000 to more than 330,000. Relatives on both sides of Michelle Obama's family made the journey from the South to Chicago.

Black politicians were particularly important figures in Chicago because they served as bridges between blacks and the white community. Blacks were segregated within the Black Belt, a compact area on Chicago's South Side, just north and west of Hyde Park. The Black Belt was a narrow strip of land seven miles long and one and a half miles wide. By 1940 more than 300,000 black Chicagoans lived there, though the area could not hold sufficient housing for them. St. Clair Drake and Horace R. Cayton, famous black social historians, called it *Black Metropolis* (the title of their book), a city within a city.

Black Metropolis or Bronzeville, as the black neighborhood was also called, was a lively place with a thriving business community, hundreds of churches, and major cultural institutions. Provident Hospital, founded in 1891 by the black surgeon Daniel Hale Williams, provided health care for blacks as well as opportunities for black professionals. The vast majority of blacks were employed, though often at low-paying jobs. They faced intense opposition from unions and others when they attempted to move into skilled employment. They paid high rents for housing in such poor condition that it could not have been rented outside the black neighborhoods. The Black Belt was so overcrowded that people were always looking for an opportunity at the edges of the neighborhood to expand its limits. Jacob Lawrence's Migration series provides a useful perspective on how the great exodus from the South was viewed in 1940. The barriers to decent employment and housing opportunities in the North are clearly illustrated. The journey as shown was fraught with difficulties. But there are no regrets, because people have come to a better place.

Once blacks settled in the North, they sought to improve their lives. In particular, they earned more money and sought to move to neighborhoods that offered better housing conditions. To keep blacks out of their neighborhoods, white Chicagoans relied primarily on racially restrictive covenants, clauses in the deeds to real estate that forbade selling the property to a black person. Some white Chicagoans were also prepared to use violence to keep black families out of their neighborhoods. Between July 1917 and March 1921, at least fifty-eight homes and offices in Chicago were bombed to keep blacks from moving into white neighborhoods.

In contrast to restricted housing and employment options, one opportunity that opened up immediately when a black person moved from the South to Chicago was the right to vote. Blacks were not just allowed to vote in Chicago; their participation was welcomed by some politicians. Ward bosses used to new immigrant groups were happy to see blacks vote—if they voted the right way—and would have resisted attempts to take away their right to vote. True, there was graft and corruption in black wards, but they existed in white wards as well. Leading politicians, including mayors, accepted support from criminals, whatever their race.

Black voting was therefore on a more equal footing with white voting than other opportunities, and politics became a special avenue of black advancement. The power of black voting was concentrated by housing segregation. The existence of a black voting bloc earned the black community representation.

In 1915 Oscar DePriest became a highly visible representative of the black community as the first black alderman elected to the Chicago City Council. DePriest had fled the Deep South at an early age. Exposure to racial violence, in his case when a black man was killed by a mob on the steps of his family's home, helped motivate his departure. He worked as a house painter in Chicago and then moved into the real estate business.

DePriest was essentially a blockbuster. He leased buildings in white areas near the borders of the existing black community and rented units to blacks at higher rents than previous white tenants had paid. He grew rich. Although wealthy, DePriest could not move to a better neighborhood because of his race. This difference between blacks and other "immigrant" groups kept black leaders in close physical proximity to the poorer members of their community.

DePriest was not a great speaker, but he was a gifted organizer and, at six feet tall, an imposing figure. He began his campaign for alderman working independently to gather support throughout his community. His initiative was greeted with enthusiasm. For DePriest, independence was a matter of expediency, not principle. When the regular Republicans bowed to the inevitable and offered their support, he accepted it.

In 1917 DePriest had to step down from the City Council when he was accused of conspiring to allow gambling houses and houses of prostitution to operate in his neighborhood, and of bribing police officers to protect these houses. The Second Ward that DePriest represented was next door to the infamous First Ward, at that time an open and notorious "red-light" district. The charges were brought against DePriest, a Republican, by a Democratic state's attorney. The practices he was accused of were common to members of both political parties, particularly before the official closing of the red-light district in 1921. Ably defended by Clarence Darrow and Edward Morris, a prominent black attorney, DePriest was cleared and resumed his political career.

As alderman, DePriest occupied a special place in the black community. Drake and Cayton, the chroniclers of *Black Me-*

tropolis, ascribed an alderman's prestige to the fact he replaced the preacher "as the key person in time of trouble." The alderman or precinct captain, unlike the preacher, could get a person on relief, out of jail, or into a job.

DePriest won election to the U.S. House of Representatives in 1928, the first black to do so in the twentieth century. He faced two additional hurdles to assuming office. The first was another indictment similar to the one he had beaten earlier; this one was later dropped by the prosecutor. The second, a possible challenge to his credentials by Southern Democrats, was evaded when Ruth Hanna McCormick, Illinois representative at large, arranged to have the oath of office administered to all the members of the Illinois delegation at once. Thus challenging DePriest's credentials would have required challenging the entire delegation.

That DePriest was elected as a Republican was taken for granted. At the time, blacks throughout the country uniformly supported the party of Lincoln the Liberator and did not immediately respond to Franklin Roosevelt's leadership. The first big wave of black voters crossing from the Republican to the Democratic party occurred in 1936. A second occurred eight years later. FDR directly addressed racial discrimination in a 1944 campaign speech in Chicago in terms the black community had waited years to hear. He clearly declared his support for equal opportunity regardless of race, creed, or color. Black voters in Chicago and elsewhere overwhelmingly changed their allegiance to the Democratic party when it was finally clear that the New Deal included everyone. Even the poorest blacks wanted their aspiration for equal rights addressed as well as their economic needs.

The change in party preference was one of the aspects of local politics that created opportunities for ambitious black politicians. Descriptions of Chicago politics naturally tend to focus on the primacy of the famed "machines" run successively by Anton Cermak, Edward Kelly, and Richard J. Daley. Mike Royko, the celebrated Chicago political columnist and sardonic critic of Richard J. Daley, presented a static, fixed portrait of Daley's organization because it suited his writer's instincts. But the machines, including Richard J. Daley's, were in fact battlegrounds of rival interests, including ethnic, political, economic, and purely personal preferences.

Consider the epic battle between Earl Dickerson, the most important black reform politician of his day, and his archrival William Dawson, a key black ally of Richard J. Daley. The superficial resemblances between Dawson and Dickerson are many. Like DePriest, both Dawson and Dickerson were born in the South. Both became lawyers and served in World War I, rising to the rank of lieutenant. Both were devoted to building a personal fortune, and each valued his membership in a black fraternity. Both served as Chicago aldermen but aspired to serve in Congress.

But Dawson and Dickerson had sharply opposing political aims. When and where each won and each lost dramatically shaped Chicago's political landscape. The effect of their contests was felt far beyond the black community. Both wanted to lead Chicago's black community, and both did in important ways. In the long run the community most affected by their struggles was Hyde Park.

*

Dickerson's life has uncanny parallels to Barack Obama's. He was born in 1891 in Mississippi. After his father's death, when he was only four years old, Dickerson was raised by a quartet of formidable women including his grandmother. When later questioned about his lack of resentment toward whites, despite his terrible encounters with racism, Dickerson would cite his grandmother. Although legally black, she was as "fair" as any white person he ever met. He traveled north to Chicago just before his sixteenth birthday. His intellectual gifts were recognized early on by a series of committed patrons who helped him get an education that few blacks received. While Obama was one of the few African-American students at an exclusive private school in Hawaii, Dickerson completed high school as the only black student at the University of Chicago's Laboratory Schools and then at Evanston Academy. About the Laboratory Schools he recalled, "I was exposed for the first time in my life to a non-segregated climate—a situation where I could share on an unequivocally equal basis the quest for education with others of different ethnic and religious backgrounds." While Obama was the first black editor-in-chief of the *Law Review* at Harvard, in 1920 Dickerson was the first black to graduate from the University of Chicago Law School. He was recognized there as a brilliant student. For his part, Dickerson later credited the university with being "the greatest inspiration of my life."

But it was his military service that made him a fighter. He was initially inspired by President Woodrow Wilson's war for democracy to volunteer for the army. Dickerson read Wilson's war message and responded with the hope that he could "take a direct part in the struggle to bring freedom and equality to the world—a world in which blacks could take their rightful place." When he was sent to a segregated officers' training school, he was appalled to find that Wilson's vision did not include American blacks. He declined a commission because of the discriminatory treatment of black officers. He later reconsidered, rejoined the army, and was commissioned a second lieutenant. Because Dickerson spoke French, he served as an interpreter for white troops. He was then transferred from that post to the command of a black infantry platoon and led soldiers in combat.

Dickerson's experience of being trained as an officer and allowed to command in combat was unusual but not unique. Ironically, his greatest future political rival, William Dawson, also had combat command experience during World War I. Thus military service, like politics, offered blacks leadership roles not available to them in other walks of life. That does not mean that black officers were treated equally with white officers.

Dickerson was bitter about the lack of opportunity for advancement for blacks in the army. Only one talented black fellow officer received an important promotion while all the black officers endured endless insults and slights. Nevertheless when Dickerson returned from combat in France, he was ready for combat in Chicago. Fighting back often paid off for Dickerson, as when he demanded and received service in Chicago restaurants or told a theater usher that refusing him admission would get the usher arrested for violating the Illinois Civil Rights Act.

Despite glowing recommendations, Dickerson was not able to find a job at a law firm when he graduated. He opened his own practice and worked for the Supreme Life Insurance Company, where he later became president. His spirited assertion of his rights and the rights of other blacks earned him a reputation for militancy. Despite building a substantial personal fortune, Dickerson was considered decidedly left-leaning. As with Obama, his reputation as a leftist was rooted in his commitment to the Constitution. Like Obama, he favored capitalism as an economic system that could in the right circumstances create opportunity for people of all races. Dickerson himself proved to be an extremely able capitalist. On behalf of Supreme Life he invented, overnight and under great pressure, a new form of lien against the value of policies already issued. This bold, creative tactic prevented the demise of his company and saved the investments of thousands of black policyholders.

Earl Dickerson took pride in his intellectual accomplishments and his ability to move comfortably among white elites, though these assets sometimes became a political liability. *(Getty Images)*

*

While Earl Dickerson was a pioneer whom modern students of black politics find sympathetic and appealing, Dawson is a troubling figure. Many commentators simply dismiss him as a hopeless party hack, a spineless toady in the service of Richard J. Daley. He was, however, at one time probably the most powerful black elected official in the United States. And although he did not criticize Daley publicly, Daley went to the trouble of destroying his position within the local Democratic party.

When Toni Preckwinkle, currently the alderman for half of Hyde Park, was a graduate student at the University of Chicago, she wrote her master's thesis on Dawson based on numerous interviews. While Dawson's rival Dickerson naturally commanded her respect, Preckwinkle struggled to understand Dawson as the black politician who actually came to power.

Dawson was born in Albany, Georgia, in 1886, so he was five years older than Dickerson. He graduated from Fisk in 1909 and moved to Chicago in 1912, then entered law school at Northwestern. After the outbreak of World War I, he volunteered for the army. Like Dickerson, he trained in a segregated officers' training school. Commissioned as a lieutenant, he commanded troops in combat and was seriously injured. Throughout his life Dawson remained deeply patriotic, but he was bitter about the inferior medical treatment he believed he had received as a black soldier. Many years later he spoke out forcefully in Congress against racial segregation in the armed forces, recalling the injuries he sustained in combat: "I went to war. . . . I led Americans in battle. . . . This left shoulder of mine is a slip joint. That would have been a good joint if hospitalization had been available and I had not been a negro American."

Once the war ended, Dawson returned to Chicago and graduated from Northwestern Law School. He began practicing law and entered politics in DePriest's organization. In 1933 he was elected alderman. According to Preckwinkle, Dawson had a maverick period as a young alderman. He challenged the city administration openly over issues of public housing for blacks and police brutality.

Dawson represented the Second Ward as alderman from 1933 until 1939. Aldermanic primaries are officially nonpartisan, but party affiliations are public knowledge and often decisive. Dawson had held aldermanic office as a Republican and in 1939 ran again as a Republican.

The Black Belt of Chicago in the 1930s was largely contained in the Second, Third, and Fourth Wards, lying close, as the numbers indicate, to the Fifth Ward that included Hyde Park. Over time this proximity would have important consequences.

Meanwhile an internal feud among white machine politicians gave Dickerson his opportunity: he ran against Dawson as a Democrat. Dawson believed he had been promised support from Edward Kelly, the Democratic mayor. But Dickerson, in addition to being popular in his own right, received regular Democratic party support and won.

After this loss Dawson joined the Democrats and ended his maverick stance. He reached out to Dickerson, and for a while the two men cooperated. Dickerson, a thoroughgoing reformer in politics, had no interest in the patronage associated with an alderman's office. He cheerfully surrendered his potential patronage to Dawson, now a Democrat, who exercised it as ward committeeman. In Chicago, ward committeeman is an officially unpaid position. But being a ward committeeman has made many Chicago politicians wealthy because of their access to patronage. Even after patronage was curtailed, committeemen remained powerful because they controlled the selection—referred to as the "slating"—of official party candidates for public office.

Dickerson's first mistake was giving Dawson his patronage. His second was believing Dawson's assurances that he would support Dickerson as a candidate for the U.S. House of Representatives. When an opening arose in 1942, Dawson put himself forward, not Dickerson, as the preferred choice for the Democratic candidate.

Dickerson was a popular figure in the black community and decided to accept the invitation posed by a "Draft Dickerson" campaign. Thus Dickerson and Dawson clashed directly as candidates for a congressional seat. During this bitterly fought campaign, Dawson used the same rhetoric against Dickerson that

Bobby Rush used against Barack Obama in 2000 when Obama sought Rush's seat in the House. Dickerson, like Obama, was derided by his opponent as a cloistered intellectual, too comfortable with white opinion makers and out of touch with the needs of poor blacks. In both cases the white opinion makers whose influence was so dangerous were clearly Hyde Parkers, affiliated with the University of Chicago.

It is easy to see the stark contrast between Bobby Rush, who served six months in prison on a weapons charge, and the Harvard-educated Obama. Dawson and Dickerson, however, were both wealthy lawyers with similar life stories. How could Dawson rail against Dickerson as a "silk stocking" University of Chicago Law School graduate when Dawson had attended Northwestern, hardly a working-class institution? It was Dickerson's pride in his University of Chicago connections and his belief that reform politics had something to offer the black community that made him vulnerable to Dawson's attacks.

The two men had entirely different attitudes toward machine politics. Dawson wanted to crack open the machine for blacks and participate on the same footing as white politicians. He saw how the machine benefited at least some whites, and he sought a share for himself and for the black community. He saw no distinction between the advancement of his personal interests and those of his people.

By contrast, Dickerson wanted to replace the machine with an open, responsive system of government. He believed that a government committed to enforcing civil rights could achieve real changes across the board. A campaign poster for Dickerson in 1942 asked voters to choose between "Jobs in Defense for All Negroes," requiring a vote for Dickerson, or "Jobs in Politics for Ward Heelers," demanding a vote for Dawson.

Victimized by Dawson's effective use of Rush-style tactics, Dickerson lost the election. Thereafter his fate as a black re-

William Dawson with Lyndon Johnson, 1960. Both men were devoted to getting the business of government done. *(Time & Life Pictures/Getty Images)*

former was similar to the fate of white reformers. He could lead a blue-ribbon commission and accept a prestigious assignment in Washington, such as serving on FDR's Fair Employment Practices Committee. But his anti-machine posture and civil rights activism prevented him from being chosen by the Democratic party. Without being slated, he could not win the seat in the U.S. House of Representatives he ardently desired.

*

In the 1955 mayoral election, Richard J. Daley received strong support from the black community, which helped him defeat Robert Merriam. The election laid the foundation of Chicago politics for the next decade. The black wards served as a mainstay for Daley in successive elections, replacing the immigrant white

wards as his most reliable source of votes. The nature and consequences of black support for Daley merit careful examination.

Daley's chief opponent in the Democratic primary in 1955
had tried to smear him as a friend of the blacks. White voters
were unmoved, but the black community responded angrily.
The *Defender*, an influential voice, editorialized on Daley's
behalf. In retrospect, it is hard not to see this as a major miscal-
culation.

Daley's success in the black wards also reflects Merriam's
failure as the Republican candidate in the 1955 mayoral election
to effectively challenge Daley for the black vote. His good-gov-
ernment message did not resonate with people still struggling
for a foothold in Chicago's job and housing markets. He did not
convince the black community that a reformed city government
would pay more attention to guarding their rights or meeting
their needs than the machine would, and there is no evidence
that he tried very hard to do so.

Daley's success in 1955 also reflected Dawson's power. By
1955 Dawson had moved beyond the local political scene. In
1942, when the South Side of Chicago sent him to the U.S.
House of Representatives as a Democrat, he became the only
black congressman in the nation. He was frequently called on
to speak on behalf of black Americans across the country. When
Adam Clayton Powell, the flamboyant black congressman from
Harlem, joined him in the House in 1944, the two made an
oddly contrasting pair. Powell, who challenged white racism at
every turn, made many enemies while the ever-accommodating
Dawson provided valuable assistance to Democratic leaders.

The difference in personal style extended to the use of the
official dining room. Dawson seldom ate there. Powell would
invite constituents to join him, then look for a table where their
presence would discomfort as many of his more prejudiced colleagues as possible.

Although Dawson had always wanted to be a congressman and was delighted to achieve this office, he continued to work hard on behalf of his lieutenants who served as aldermen and ward committeemen. He never lost his focus on Chicago politics. In 1955 he was thus the most powerful black politician in Chicago and one of the most powerful politicians in the city.

In the mayoral contest Dawson threw his support wholeheartedly to Daley. Dawson had played a key role in dumping Daley's predecessor, Martin Kennelly, whom Dawson despised. It was not Dawson's style to look for specific guarantees from Daley on behalf of the black community or even to judge Daley's racial attitudes. Dawson knew his political clout was crucial to Daley's victory, and he expected to benefit accordingly. He believed his greater influence would benefit the entire black community.

Daley did reward the black community for its support. He created additional black wards; he sponsored black judges. The number of black aldermen increased, and they received important committee assignments on the City Council. In return, the black aldermen sponsored by Daley remained silent in the council and never raised awkward questions about race. The independent black alderman Charles Chew derided them as the "silent six."

For a while Dawson's influence in the City Council was strong. He worked hard to extend his power beyond his own ward. He was seen by the press as a mini-me black version of Mayor Richard J. Daley and was often referred to as "Boss" Dawson. But in Richard J. Daley's Chicago there was room for only one boss. Daley reached beyond the recognized black politicians to the black elites when he wanted help. This strategy allowed him to bypass and discredit the established black politicians, including those who had helped him to power. In the end, Daley turned on Dawson and stripped him of his city patronage. One observer, who watched Dawson lose this battle,

described how "there was no public disgrace, just a surgical re-
moval of multi-ward power from Dawson to Daley."

Dawson retained his congressional seat for twenty-eight
years, until 1970. During that time his influence in the House of
Representatives continued to grow, even after 1955 as his power
in Chicago eroded.

Beyond Richard J. Daley's treatment of an individual black
leader lies the much larger issue of how black Chicagoans fared
under his administration. He made every effort to retain and
reinforce the city's segregated housing pattern, which in turn
limited black access to quality public education. He discouraged
any attempt to challenge racial discrimination in employment.
He made the disastrous decision to build massive high-rise public housing projects in a handful of black wards.

In the 1960s and 1970s Chicago lost thousands of good-
paying jobs in the stockyards and in manufacturing. Losses on
this scale would have been a serious blow to blacks regardless of
the political leadership. But the unequal division of resources
and opportunities, particularly in education, left the black community poorly prepared to cope with these traumatic changes.

In this context, Dawson's success in Chicago politics and
Dickerson's failure are crucial. Given his intellectual abilities
and grasp of policy, Dickerson might have made a great congressman instead of a useful one. But other consequences of
Dickerson's loss to Dawson far outweigh their respective potential as congressmen. Dawson, as the most powerful leader of the
growing black community, was willing, even eager, for Richard
J. Daley's leadership. Dickerson would never have supported
Daley as Dawson did. Once installed in office, Daley was difficult to influence and impossible to dislodge.

In 1947, five years after his defeat by Dawson, Dickerson
moved to Hyde Park. He never ran for office from Hyde Park.
Instead he helped build an interracial community that eventu-

ally provided Barack Obama with a unique racial and political setting. Dickerson had yearned to enter the U.S. House of Representatives and rise above the Chicago City Council, where his colleagues cared more about patronage than substantive political issues. But he could not defeat Dawson, and in his turn Obama could not defeat Bobby Rush. Yet the prize they both sought was in Washington, D.C., and the work to which Dickerson devoted part of his later life in Hyde Park helped Obama immeasurably.

Hyde Park was ready to become an integrated neighborhood. That would expand its role in Chicago politics and give Hyde Park's call for reform new urgency and meaning.

FIVE
CREATING A RACIALLY
BALANCED COMMUNITY

After World War II, race emerged from the secluded realms of scholarly research and philanthropic endeavors to center stage in everyday life in Hyde Park. Blacks had moved into communities in the South and West Sides of Chicago as part of the "Great Migration" from the South. In the 1940s land clearance near Hyde Park for large public and private housing projects displaced residents and increased the demand for the neighborhood's residential units. Large numbers of black Chicagoans seeking better housing appeared ready and able to move into Hyde Park. One remaining barrier was the racially restrictive covenants used in the deeds to Hyde Park homes.

After Earl Dickerson lost the election for the congressional seat in 1942, he turned his attention back to his community. His desire to advance black Americans' civil rights in every possible arena naturally led him to oppose racially restrictive covenants. He had already brought suit on behalf of Carl Hansberry, who tried to buy a home in the Woodlawn community south of Hyde Park. Dickerson fought the case to the U.S. Supreme Court, where it was heard on October 25, 1940. He won on technical grounds, so the issue of whether a restrictive covenant violated the Constitution was not settled. Nonetheless the case opened up a broad area of the solidly white South Side to black home owners. The case also made a deep impression on Hansberry's ten-year-old daughter Lorraine, who later wrote the Broadway hit *A Raisin in the Sun*, about a black family's struggle to buy a house in a white neighborhood.

Dickerson wanted blacks to be able to live wherever they chose. He moved into Hyde Park in 1947, the same year that Sara Spurlark and her husband bought a home in the neighborhood.

The debate about whether a stable interracial community was feasible gained urgency in 1948 when the Supreme Court struck down any use of racially restrictive covenants in real estate deeds. In 1948 blacks had not begun moving into Hyde Park in any numbers, but their arrival seemed inevitable. The few pioneers, including Dickerson and Spurlark, could be easily accommodated. But if it was legal for Dickerson and Spurlark to live in Hyde Park, what about the thousands of black families looking for a decent place to live?

Did this mean, as it had in nearby communities such as Oakwood, northwest of Hyde Park–Kenwood, that a total racial transformation was inevitable? Many people thought so.

It was clear that black people would move into Hyde Park–Kenwood if they could, because racial discrimination limited their housing options elsewhere. White people could move to other areas of the city or to the suburbs, which were closed to blacks. The issue was whether white residents could be retained for the long run if black residents moved in. When significant numbers of blacks began to arrive in Hyde Park and Kenwood in the early 1950s, community organizers tried to persuade white families not to move. Organizers argued that if white families stayed, the neighborhood could achieve integration.

The impulse to integrate the community received crucial support from a wide variety of religious organizations. A number of faith-based groups had concluded over the years that integration would provide both an alternative for black families presently forced to live in slum conditions in other neighborhoods and a more ethical basis for community life. Churches and synagogues in Hyde Park had an unusually long record of interfaith cooperation. Moreover race relations was an excellent vehicle for interfaith efforts. Working for integration allowed religious groups to focus on an important topic while ignoring potentially divisive doctrinal differences.

The University of Chicago, whatever the progressive views of some of its faculty, staff, and students, had no institutional commitment to the creation of a stable interracial community. In fact the university's unannounced policy was to fund the Hyde Park Planning Association, a loose confederation of large hotel operators and university administrators devoted to keeping racially restrictive covenants intact.

As a result of intense discussion, by the late 1940s a consensus had emerged among Hyde Parkers to open the neighborhood to black families. In 1949 concerned citizens formed the Hyde Park–Kenwood Community Conference (HPKCC) to create a stable integrated community with high standards for housing. A Quaker group helped lay the foundation for the conference's work by convening public meetings about race relations. The Reverend Leslie Pennington, a Unitarian minister, served as chairman at the conference's first public meeting. Local synagogues sent delegations.

Important black leaders, including Earl Dickerson, agreed that a stable integrated neighborhood was desirable. Dickerson was a founding member of the conference. His presence and that of other prominent blacks was deeply reassuring to progressive whites.

Herbert Thelen, who taught in the University of Chicago's Department of Education and who had special expertise in group dynamics, attended the first meeting of the HPKCC with a number of his students. He helped organize the block groups that spread throughout Hyde Park and Kenwood from 1950 on and made the difference in achieving a racially balanced community.

Block groups met in people's homes and encouraged white families to sit tight and resist blockbusting pressure to sell their homes. In this scenario, a real estate broker would sell one home on a block to a black family, then frighten the remaining owners into selling at bargain prices. To build morale, block group leaders encouraged neighbors to focus on small, solvable urban problems such as an untidy alley. Achieving modest victories built a sense of solidarity and confirmed the importance of acting as a group.

In his memoir, Barack Obama notes in his description of racial change in general that white people were often frightened by tactics such as blockbusting, but he fails to acknowledge the fear of blacks that allowed such tactics to succeed. The block groups of Hyde Park–Kenwood were willing to share their community with black families and interracial families, but they expected newcomers to share their values. Unlike Obama, the block group leaders acknowledged the basic racial fear behind the immediate jitters. This honesty allowed the block groups to mobilize people to tackle local concerns and think beyond their fears.

The block groups were loosely organized under the wings of the Hyde Park–Kenwood Community Conference. The conference's reach within the community in the 1950s was remarkable. Membership was unevenly distributed, and the level of interest varied. Still, at its height participation in the conference included one of every five households. This base of support allowed the conference to field seven paid staff members and operate an office.

The university and the community agreed on the need for more information. The neighborhood that had dispatched so many people to study other parts of the city now studied itself very thoroughly; the chosen method was a detailed survey of housing conditions and neighborhood retail districts. Beyond the physical state of the community, the survey aimed to understand how satisfied residents were with their surroundings and what improvements they wanted. The tabulated results of the survey were later used to support the designation of parcels of land in clearance and urban renewal projects.

When Mrs. Oswelda Badal moved to a new home in Hyde Park after her marriage in 1950, she was surprised that a neighbor rang the doorbell and interviewed her for the survey. She went on to work in the city's departments of Urban Renewal and Planning. At eighty-two and still a Hyde Park resident, she recalls this period as one when she was truly proud of her neighbors who assessed their needs, planned changes, and stood up for their vision of what should happen in their community.

Despite the remarkable level of community mobilization, there was concern that lower-middle-class and working-class blacks were reluctant to join the block groups. But Victor Townes, a black dining-car steward, proved an exceptionally effective block group leader.

This massive effort to begin integration through community organization was initially successful. Hyde Parkers, however, differed sharply about how to maintain integration. At the core of the disagreement was whether the creation of a stable racial balance would require an urban renewal program.

Urban renewal refers to more than one government-funded program. The state as well as the federal government funded it. The important points to remember are that urban renewal included but was not limited to demolition, and that because it required the use of tax dollars, there were rules to follow and goals to meet. Broadly stated, receiving urban renewal funding required the preparation of a comprehensive plan for demolition, development, and rehabilitation. The plan would have to be approved by the Chicago City Council, which would depend on Mayor Richard J. Daley's wishes.

Attitudes toward urban renewal were deeply influenced by what people thought about the physical state of the neighborhood. What shape was Hyde Park in when urban renewal was proposed?

By 1950 Hyde Park and Kenwood were predominately middle-class communities with some poorer and some wealthier residents. Like many city neighborhoods of that era, they were more economically diverse than the new suburbs that were beginning to attract Chicagoans. The largest ethnic group, about 40 percent, were Jews of European descent. Japanese Americans had arrived in significant numbers in 1942 from the western United States.

Between 1940 and 1950 the population of Hyde Park–Kenwood had grown by almost 10 percent. But there had been little new housing construction in this period, partly because of the war but also because there was not much vacant land. New dwelling units were created through the division of existing units into smaller units, often illegally. After the war, temporary housing for students under the GI Bill was erected near the University of Chicago campus.

Thus the neighborhood was showing its age. After World War II many new communities were being built successfully outside major cities. White families were moving to these suburbs. The perception was that Hyde Park was deteriorating, at least in places, and was therefore less attractive to white families who could consider the suburbs.

Were white people moving to the suburbs to get away from black people, or for the amenities? If at least some were moving for the amenities, what specific new amenities would persuade them to stay? Proponents of urban renewal argued that it was the best available means of paying for new amenities—including parks, improved shopping, and better housing—that might induce whites to stay.

The renewal of Hyde Park–Kenwood was challenging because it incorporated and eliminated parts of existing communities. This ambitious project was undertaken because of the neighborhood's unique assets, including the lakefront location, the parks, much of the housing stock, and institutions including the University of Chicago.

Some community leaders questioned the need for urban renewal projects, particularly the demolition of buildings that could be rehabilitated. They advocated maintaining a racial balance through strict enforcement of open-housing laws and the encouragement of good property maintenance. The city had no open-housing ordinance at this time. Integration in Hyde Park–Kenwood was thus achieved by local action, not through external pressure such as a court decree. But the community did work for better housing code enforcement and better property maintenance.

Those who favored urban renewal argued that even a well-maintained community facing racial change could not attract public or private investment without an urban renewal program. They insisted that black migration to the South Side had ended purely private profit-driven investment. Hyde Park still lay on the lakefront, its housing stock was largely intact, the university was reaching new heights of prestige having recently split the atom, and the commercial district was far livelier than it is today. Nevertheless Hyde Park could easily have suffered the same disinvestment as other formerly attractive neighborhoods. For example, not a single market-rate house was built in North Kenwood, immediately north of Hyde Park–Kenwood, between World War II and 1995.

Urban renewal was chosen. The decision changed the neighborhood but did not end the debate. After World War II many new communities were successfully built outside major cities. The creation of Hyde Park–Kenwood was far more challenging because it incorporated and eliminated parts of existing communities.

But the extent of the demolition should not be exaggerated. Hyde Park did look different after urban renewal, but other city neighborhoods that were not part of urban renewal experienced far more demolition and far less investment. Substantial investment came to Hyde Park, including dollars for rehabilitation and repair through urban renewal.

When home building began again in Hyde Park in the 1950s and 1960s, construction was financed with federal money. Public money poured into the newly emerging community of Hyde Park–Kenwood through the adoption of major urban renewal projects. More than $400 million in public funds paid for the acquisition and demolition of buildings, major infrastructure changes, new parks, and the construction of new shopping centers and hundreds of new homes, including apartments and single-family houses. Community organizers put enormous pressure on private property owners to maintain and upgrade their buildings. Some private investment appeared, including money from the University of Chicago, but what attracted that money as well as city and state funds were the substantial federal dollars. Federal funding provided a range of assistance: after building new homes, urban renewal offered middle-class families federally guaranteed loans with which to buy them.

The University of Chicago was deeply involved in urban renewal and benefited greatly from this public investment. At the time the university, like other anchor institutions in the community, faced two alternatives. It could move or stay. In 1966 George Williams College, an institution affiliated with the YMCA, moved from Hyde Park to Downers Grove, a suburb of Chicago. Moving was probably never a viable option for the University of Chicago because of its existing, massive investment in the community. But others disagree, and the question certainly hung in the air for several years. Even if the university remained, the faculty and staff could have chosen to live elsewhere and commute to campus, a situation increasingly common at older urban universities.

The Hyde Park–Kenwood block groups convinced people to stay. They did not expect that urban renewal would bring them new amenities; they stayed because their neighbors asked them to stay, and because they believed their neighbors would stay as well. People were receptive to the block groups' message partly because they liked where they lived and partly because they were attracted by the prospect of integration.

The block group strategy was a crisis-driven, short-term response to the arrival of black people in the community. It was undertaken with funds raised in the community. But in order to achieve lasting racial stability, many community leaders believed they needed larger amounts of money than they could raise locally.

Raising more money meant partnering with the University of Chicago, the largest and most important landowner in the community. The university was committed to urban renewal; the HPKCC did not have the capacity to manage the detailed work of urban renewal planning. In 1954 the university set up a planning unit and thereafter relied on its professional planners to determine exactly what urban renewal should look like. The HPKCC leadership deferred to the planners on many questions, especially relating to specific land-use decisions.

This transition was not easy. The HPKCC and the community institutions allied with it created an atmosphere favorable to urban renewal and the use of specialists. But the conference prided itself on its democratic structure, and its leaders wanted important public participation in the entire planning process. Literally hundreds of meetings were conducted to promote urban renewal and consider proposals in detail. The division of labor between the block groups and the technical experts was largely according to gender: the experts were usually men while the block groups were often led by women.

Despite the HPKCC's commitment to urban renewal and its willingness to accept expert guidance, the University of Chicago wanted a community organization under its direct control. In 1952 the university founded the South East Chicago Commission (SECC), which emerged as the university's chosen vehicle for community participation in urban renewal. Although Hyde Parkers who resented the university's influence in the community bitterly attacked the SECC as an ersatz community organization, created for the university's convenience, it did attract community support in its early years. In 1954, for example, the university provided only $10,000 of the commission's $45,000 budget. The remainder came from the community, including donations from fourteen hundred individuals and institutions. In the same year the Field Foundation gave the SECC and the university a $100,000 grant to plan urban renewal, bearing out the expectation that the university's involvement was essential in securing substantial external funding.

The SECC had a special focus on law enforcement in addition to other neighborhood issues. Fear of crime was a respectable proxy for fear of racial change. Concern about crime was the most effective means of mobilizing the community. At the same time emphasizing crime prevention through effective enforcement was acceptable to an increasingly racially diverse community. Black residents also feared crime. The SECC worked with the university's police force to assist victims of crime, prevent crime, and ensure public awareness of crime patterns. This effort was a two-edged sword. While the SECC's efforts certainly reassured Hyde Parkers that crime was being taken seriously, the sheer amount of information available about crime sometimes convinced people that crime was more prevalent than it actually was.

Julian Levi, whose brother Edward later became president of the University of Chicago, was the hard-charging director of the South East Chicago Commission. He spared no one, including the city government and federal officials, from harsh criticism. He was a relentless champion of the projects he favored. Julia Abrahamson, the first executive director of the HPKCC, recognized both the polarizing effect Julian Levi had on the community and the fact that the difficulties extended beyond him. "Some of the university policy makers," she wrote, "had little contact with the community fears and feelings that conference leaders experienced daily. It was naturally hard for them to foresee the intensity of the reaction to the university's plans, or to weigh heavily enough the judgment of conference leaders on this point."

Julian Levi, right, inspecting a slum building, 1954. He protected the University of Chicago with relentless zeal. *(Time & Life Pictures/Getty Images)*

The planning experts were dedicated to the idea that the quality of people's lives flowed from their physical surroundings. They saw the enemy as "blight," which surrounded a community and penetrated it along pathways provided by substandard buildings, greedy landlords, and unwholesome businesses. (In fact "blight" defined inadequate conditions, such as homes that lacked bathrooms or poorly maintained structures. Contemporary descriptions make blight sound like a virus.) Eliminating blight required land clearance and the rehabilitation of buildings.

The planners had little inherent respect for the "urban" part of their undertaking. The ideal was suburban. Any celebration of urban living that would resonate with today's readers is missing from the planning documents. The planners list the major institutions as assets. They have no praise for any feature of urban life such as walkability, variety, or even access to cultural events such as concerts. The planners feared that the white middle class they wished to retain would be attracted to rivals such as the prosperous suburb of Highland Park. They did not fear Lincoln Park, a stylish, upscale neighborhood on the North Side of Chicago, brimming with the amenities Hyde Park lacks. In 1958 a neighborhood like Lincoln Park was not anticipated.

The community the planners created was racially balanced, overwhelmingly middle class, and far less populous than the community they started with. By 1950 the population of Hyde Park–Kenwood had increased to 71,689, up from 65,273 in 1940. From 1956 to 1960 the demolition of buildings and the relocation of their inhabitants reduced the population by more than 9 percent, to 64,819. The population continued to decline after 1960. The drop between 1960 and 1970 was significant, from 64,819 to 46,035, as demolition and relocation were completed. Hyde Park–Kenwood's population thereafter declined steadily, falling to 46,035 in 1970, 45,377 in 1980, 41,161 in 1990, and then posting a modest increase to 42,749 in 2000.

The percentage of blacks in the neighborhood grew significantly during this period. In 1940 the nonwhite population of Hyde Park–Kenwood was 1.5 percent. By 1950 it was about 6 percent. And then the pace of change accelerated greatly. In 1956 the nonwhite percentage had risen to 36.7 percent. This increase persisted despite clearances and relocations, and in 1960 the population of Hyde Park–Kenwood was 47 percent black. The black population was clearly more than the handful that critics of urban renewal said were allowed in. Substantial numbers of middle-class blacks were looking for decent housing.

In 1970 the percentage of the population that was black had fallen to 38.12 percent, but in succeeding decades the figure increased to 46 percent (1980), 47 percent (1990), and 46 percent (2000). The dip between 1960 and 1970 appears to reflect the popularity of both new and existing housing with whites in the 1960s, and probably also the fact that whites still had more money to invest in housing. The essential point is that substantial numbers of both whites and blacks sold and bought homes without the prospect that either group would disappear from the community.

After 1990 it was possible to track more easily the growth of the Asian community in Hyde Park–Kenwood, which has increased continually. Asians are perceived as neutral in discussions of racial balance. They add diversity, but their presence does not threaten either blacks or whites.

*

Urban renewal in Hyde Park–Kenwood embraced multiple projects. The success or failure of individual ventures depended on the caliber of community participation in the planning process. The university and the planners looked to the commission and the conference to manage community opinion and win acceptance for their proposals. If the community heartily disliked the project, it was rejected. One example, the South West Hyde Park Neighborhood Corporation Project, was a relatively small proposal organized and planned entirely by the University of Chicago under a state-authorized program. St. Clair Drake, who lived in Hyde Park–Kenwood and taught at Roosevelt University, had worked on behalf of the HPKCC. But he led the charge against this project on the grounds that it ignored the needs of the community, especially blacks, by building housing only for university students and employees. Moreover the housing to be torn down was not obviously deteriorated, particularly in comparison with other buildings that were being demolished. The targeted buildings housed many black families who considered their homes an improvement over what had previously been available to them. Drake's criticisms resonated with the wider community, and the project was abandoned amid an uproar that damaged relationships between the university and community members for years.

By contrast, an urban renewal proposal for northwest Hyde Park succeeded. Planning for this proposal actually began in the community. Prominent Hyde Parkers, including the University of Chicago's Maynard Krueger, organized a not-for-profit corporation. Their work is often cited by defenders of the urban renewal process, as a sizable number of black residents participated, among them Earl Dickerson. The project itself was not very sexy, and a great deal of time was spent determining exactly how much land would be cleared for institutional purposes. But the negotiations between university officials, planners, and the community were marked by civility and a recognition of the validity of each other's concerns.

The final and by far the largest project was the Hyde Park– Kenwood Urban Renewal Project, which covered 855.8 acres— almost the entire neighborhood excluding only the University of Chicago campus, other project areas already described, and the Illinois Central railroad right-of-way. Most of the buildings included were designated for rehabilitation, not demolition.

Just over 100 acres of land in Hyde Park–Kenwood were cleared and divided as follows: nearly 43 acres for housing, with a maximum of 1,949 dwelling units; 8.1 acres for commercial reuse; 17.2 acres for institutional uses; 8.6 acres for private parking; and just over 28 acres for public agencies, with the largest shares going to the Board of Education and for streets and alleys.

Richard J. Daley, right, breaking ground for urban renewal in Hyde Park with developers William Zeckendorf, Sr., and William Zeckendorf, Jr. Daley's wholehearted support of urban renewal was not enough to win the loyalty of many Hyde Parkers. *(University of Chicago Library, Special Collections Research Center)*

Both families and individuals were dislocated by urban renewal. City employees tracked the relocation of families due to demolition and judged the quality of the buildings where residents were rehoused. In regard to the first project, surprisingly, most of the 925 families relocated (55 percent) were white, 28 percent were black, and the rest Hispanic and Asian. Of the 531 single individuals who had to relocate, 81 percent were white.

The subsequent largest Hyde Park–Kenwood urban renewal project displaced many more people, including 3,092 families and 2,392 single individuals. The vast majority of the families, 2,234, were black while 59 percent of the single people were white. Almost all these people moved into what the city considered standard as opposed to substandard housing. Standard housing at this time included public housing. Among the families that moved into public housing, there was a great racial disparity. Fifteen white and 484 nonwhite families moved into public housing. Altogether 18,991 people were moved, 35 percent of whom were white. Thirty percent were reported to have moved to a new home within the community.

Relocation did not occur only as a result of demolition. Urban renewal also included active enforcement of building codes, which further reduced the number of available units. Preventing buildings, both single-family homes and apartment buildings, from being divided into smaller units was a key issue for the conference and later the commission. It was especially important in South Kenwood as the area included many large, freestanding houses on oversized lots. Similarly sized houses in Hyde Park stood on smaller lots, and those closer to the university had often been converted to institutional use, which alarmed no one. The Kenwood Open House Committee concentrated on the preservation of South Kenwood, particularly its largest homes. The approach was double-barreled. The organizers sought to prevent landlords from cutting up the mansions or to force them to restore them as single-family homes. They also recruited people as residents who could maintain the buildings as single-family homes, offering welcoming receptions and tours.

While the members of the Open House Committee organized recruitment, others directed enforcement. Julian Levi served as an assistant corporation counsel without pay to prosecute the owners of illegal rooming houses in South Kenwood. One of the houses he protected would later belong to Barack and Michelle Obama. They moved from that house to the White House.

Many critics have claimed that Hyde Park used urban renewal to exclude the poor from the neighborhood. When the Hyde Park urban renewal ordinance came up for consideration in the Chicago City Council, the issue of public housing was front and center. Monsignor John Egan, a respected Catholic priest who was a passionate advocate for the poor, testified against the ordinance specifically because he believed it did not include enough public housing. The next day numerous Hyde Parkers representing a wide range of local organizations rebutted his testimony. The community members who united to oppose Father Egan were among the people who were most committed to integration and most needed to see it through.

In fact little public housing was built. Even scattered-site housing, mandated by the City Council as a condition of approval of the urban renewal ordinance, drew opposition. Edwin Rothschild, a Hyde Park attorney who headed the Hyde Park–Kenwood Conservation Community Council, the land-use planning arm established under urban renewal, tried to lead the way. He had the CCC suggest six units of public housing near the block where he resided. They were built and stand today, set back from Dorchester Avenue between Fifty-fifth and Fifty-sixth Streets, in the shade of large trees. One other set of six units and public housing for the elderly were built along Fifty-fifth Street. While none of these buildings has been a problem, no further public housing was built.

Still, the neighborhood continued to provide a substantial number of housing units for poor people, subsidized by grants to landlords through the Section Eight program. Section Eight subsidies limit the amount of rent people must pay if they meet federal income guidelines. These subsidies may be paid to owners of new or existing housing. One tenant in a subsidized apartment may live next to another tenant paying market rent for an identical apartment.

In 1990, of the 22,333 housing units in the 18 census tracts composing Hyde Park–Kenwood, there were 2,005 subsidized units, or 9 percent of the total. None of the census tracts were without subsidized units, and none had a majority of subsidized units. The existence of these units contributed to the income diversity that continued to characterize Hyde Park–Kenwood. If other middle-class areas of the city had the same percentage of subsidized units as Hyde Park–Kenwood, poor people would be much more evenly distributed throughout the city and would have access to better schools, shopping, and other amenities.

At the time urban renewal in Hyde Park was debated, public housing was generally considered an excellent alternative for poor people, especially working families. The huge high-rises that later deteriorated into massive, crime-ridden slums had not yet been built elsewhere. The Hyde Park urban renewal ordinance was voted on in 1958. The massive Robert Taylor Homes, the largest of Chicago's public housing projects, would not open until 1962.

Despite its scarcity, public housing would not have strengthened integration in Hyde Park. While for many years publicly funded housing in Chicago served the needs of working-class whites, the benefits of safe, well-built public housing were extended to blacks only via the totally segregated Ida B. Wells development, north of Hyde Park–Kenwood. Swallowing their resentment of segregation, black leaders praised the project because it provided decent housing to a community mired in slums. In addition, its construction provided employment for black professionals and skilled black labor.

In the 1940s and 1950s disastrous attempts were made to integrate public housing in Chicago. As the buildings were con- structed and managed by the government, it might seem relatively easy to insist that they be integrated. But these attempts failed because whites who lived in adjacent areas frequently attacked black tenants and damaged the new housing. The city lacked the political will to halt these attacks and enforce integration.

Thus if a large amount of public housing had been built in Hyde Park, it is unlikely that it would have helped maintain a racial balance. Obviously there were thousands of poor black people who would have eagerly moved into public housing in Hyde Park. But where would the poor whites have come from?

In the 1980s I served on the board of the DARE building, the first apartment building in Hyde Park in which every unit was covered by a Section Eight subsidy. The building, opened in 1986, is the functional equivalent of public housing. It is relatively small at twenty-four units and is conveniently and desirably located near shopping and public transportation. Residents must have income below limits set by federal law and may not be charged more than 30 percent of their income as rent. The building was especially designed to accommodate the physically handicapped.

The not-for-profit group that developed the building assured the community that handicapped-accessible housing was in such high demand that tenants would be racially diverse and carefully vetted. As a member of the board of directors I learned two things. First, keeping the building free of drug dealing was an enormous challenge because tenants who had become physically handicapped during their career as dealers remained in that line of work when they moved into the building. They continued to sell drugs and terrorized other tenants. We regained control of the building through evictions. Second, even a safe, well-maintained, subsidized, handicap-accessible building with a majority of black tenants attracts few white applicants. Thus while a public housing project that was small and actively managed could serve its tenants well, it would not contribute to integration.

*

Urban renewal planners attacked blight with land clearance and the rehabilitation of buildings. But creating a new, restructured community required more, including different patterns of land use, more open space, less density, compact and contained commercial districts, a tightly controlled traffic pattern, new construction, and ample parking. Many of these features of urban planning have been abandoned by contemporary experts and have come under searching criticism. They reflect suburban planning, and in the long run all have proved disastrous.

The pocket parks installed in Hyde Park became a nuisance and were often the site of petty criminal activity. No one wanted to pay to park on the private lots originally envisioned. The surface parking lots broke up commercial areas. The restricted traffic patterns stifled commercial activity and inconvenienced people; they deliberately made both access to the community and travel within the community slower and more limited. Some residents believed they prevented crime, others perceived the barriers to the usual flow of traffic as racially isolating, and thus they were resented by the residents of nearby black neighborhoods.

People who lived and worked in Hyde Park were angered by the significantly smaller commercial districts within the community. This grievance endures because the business sector has not revived, and its weakness is probably current Hyde Parkers' chief complaint about their community.

Urban renewal produced a community of fewer than fifty thousand people, so clearly the neighborhood was much less dense than it had been. Little attention was paid at the time to the problems that would follow from this lack of density. Over time it became clear that reduced density made it harder to revive the retail sector and sustain other institutions. Meanwhile, despite the failure to build public housing, many poor people remain in the neighborhood.

The Jewish community of Hyde Park–Kenwood provides a dramatic example of the consequences of reduced density. Urban renewal halved the Jewish population, which declined from fifteen thousand people in 1950 to about seven thousand afterward. Most of those who left went to the suburbs. Over time this smaller community in Hyde Park had difficulty sustaining its synagogues, schools, and other institutions, some of which closed, consolidated, or moved. Grief over the departures of some institutions was balanced by the knowledge that Hyde Park soon became the only surviving viable South Side Jewish community. For example, South Shore, a largely Jewish community south of Hyde Park, once had far more synagogues and Jewish schools. But if Obama had chosen to live in one of South Shore's elegant homes, he would never have found himself opposite a synagogue, as every temple had closed or moved away years earlier.

During urban renewal, Hyde Park lost 641 businesses, more than half its original total. By 1968 only 233 of the remaining businesses were still operating. The new shopping centers did not accommodate many of the existing businesses. Of the 61 businesses operating in the new shopping centers, only 23 were displaced businesses that had relocated.

This major devastation in the number of retail businesses and premises for shops was not an unintended consequence. Nor was it intended to be a short-term "cost" of rebuilding. Eighty percent of the property fronting on streets that had been formerly zoned commercial were rezoned for residential or institutional use. The urban renewal planners particularly distrusted commercial sectors of the community. In their final report they had concluded that "the most blighted sections of Hyde Park–Kenwood are nearly all around commercial districts. 47th Street, 55th Street, and Cottage Grove are notorious examples. Hyde Park's newest embryonic slum, centering on 53rd and Woodlawn, is also starting around a commercial nucleus."

To modern observers this perspective is counterintuitive. The absence of ordinary businesses is a key signal that a neighborhood is indeed poor and isolated. Urban renewal planners succeeded in removing forty-three taverns from Hyde Park–Kenwood. Liquor has remained a favorite target for both the city and those who say Not in My Back Yard. But urban renewal also displaced merchants selling consumer goods and professionals providing services to largely middle-class clients. Today both the City of Chicago and its neighborhoods try hard and often unsuccessfully to attract and retain exactly this type of business. The University of Chicago has spent endless time and money seeking to expand Hyde Park–Kenwood's retail options. After uprooting so many businesses to create a community that would attract its faculty and staff, the university is persistently and vocally criticized by these individuals for the lack of shopping and dining options.

Why were so many functioning businesses sacrificed? The planners were convinced that most people would shop by car and that they would prefer "concentrated" shopping centers built around parking lots. Planners believed that one store of each type would be sufficient in the neighborhood, particularly as they predicted that much shopping would be done in downtown Chicago. Apart from these considerations, they had a deep-seated desire for control: no retail district could be allowed to begin blight again.

Attention was first focused on the plight of the small retailers rather than their customers. In 1955 Alderman Leon Despres testified before a congressional subcommittee that the problem was that "of giving justice to the small displaced and dispossessed business tenant."

After urban renewal the neighborhood launched a series of experiments to counter the loss of so many businesses. Apart from concerns about social justice, people wanted more places to shop and greater choices. One response was the Kimbark Plaza Shopping Center on Fifty-third Street. A group of merchants displaced by urban renewal built themselves a strip shopping center that opened in 1963. Unable to relocate within the limited space of the new shopping centers, despite their excellent individual records of profitability, the merchants banded together and built the plaza as a commercial condominium. Special legislation was passed to allow them to purchase land cleared under urban renewal on favorable terms, despite objections from chain stores. They obtained a combination of private financing and Small Business Administration loans. Their spirit and commitment to continuing to serve the neighborhood attracted support from the community and local politicians. While the organizers involved ran independent operations, not chain stores, they were not "small" businessmen running tiny, quaint shops. They were successful and tenacious business and professional men who operated profitably and continued to do so.

Unfortunately the spirit of cooperation that created the plaza also limited its ability to shift direction when necessary. The desire to treat all investors fairly led to the adoption of the rare and unwieldy commercial condominium form of ownership. Later the owners could not reach consensus on a strategy to deal with new challenges and aging buildings. Once both prosperous and a source of community pride, the Kimbark Plaza has deteriorated, and the university has acquired a controlling interest in it.

Another response to urban renewal was the development of Harper Court, a shopping center that aimed to house small, locally owned businesses, especially artisans. Harper Court was built on land, cleared under urban renewal, next to Fifty-third Street, including a section of Harper Avenue that was closed to traffic. Muriel Beadle, a determined, vibrant woman who easily overshadowed her husband George, the famous geneticist who served at the time as president of the University of Chicago, spearheaded the project with lively, amateur zeal. Community members responded enthusiastically to the concept, buying bonds to support construction.

Opened in 1965, the Court was an attractive place, drawing crowds to shops and restaurants as well as outdoor events. It tried to replace artisans that had been displaced by charging some creative new small businesses lower rents. But few artisans or small businesses displaced by urban renewal ever rented there. Only Acasa Book and Gift Store was relocated to Harper Court from a demolished building on Fifty-fifth Street. When I was eight or nine years old, Acasa was one of the most important places in the world. The owner chose every item on sale according to her personal quirky aesthetic, selling beautifully illustrated books, elegant note cards, calendars, and a gorgeous collection of finely made dollhouse dolls imported from Germany. I saved my allowance faithfully to purchase, one doll at a time, a family to live in my dollhouse. Acasa exemplified the delightful eccentricity a city can harbor but that cannot be planned into existence.

Over time the Court fell into disrepair. The poorly built buildings could not be altered to accommodate changing standards that included stroller and wheelchair accessibility. The restaurants continued to flourish, but the retail spaces were too small and too odd to accommodate the merchants the community hoped to attract. As with Kimbark Plaza, the Court's board, composed of well-meaning local residents, failed to agree on a strategy for change. The University of Chicago bought the property in 2008, intending to demolish it.

When evaluating Hyde Park's efforts to improve its retail sector, it is important to remember the lingering corporate racism that contributed to a difficult situation. The stores that both black and white Hyde Parkers wanted to shop at often did not wish to locate in what they perceived as a black community.

One bright spot in Hyde Park's retail saga is the survival of first-rate bookstores. My father, Morris Janowitz, believed that good bookstores were as necessary to a university as a good library. He persuaded Edward Shils, an eminent sociologist, and Saul Bellow, the famous novelist who taught at the University of Chicago, to join with him to form the Friends of the Hyde Park Booksellers. They loaned Michael Powell three thousand dollars to start Powell's Books. He repaid them promptly. My father walked through the neighborhood every evening. When he noticed a burnt-out commercial building at the corner of Fifty-seventh Street and Harper Avenue, he recognized an opportunity. In 1971 the same trio helped Powell's and O'Gara's, another Hyde Park bookstore, move into the building.

In 1979 Powell moved his business to Portland, Oregon, where it grew into a local landmark with a national reputation. His Hyde Park store passed into the competent hands of Brad Jonas. From his base in Hyde Park, Jonas built a large and innovative bookselling business. He is the cofounder of CIROBE (the Chicago International Remainder and Overstock Exposition), an enormously successful trade fair. O'Gara's and Powell's remain on Fifty-seventh Street and along with 57th Street Books offer a serious book buyer a range of pleasant options. Thus the Friends of the Hyde Park Booksellers helped two anchor retail stores prosper in the community and prepared the way for substantial commercial activity. Notably, no economists were involved.

Improvements for the public schools, promised by the urban renewal plan, never materialized. Only two public schools, Murray and Shoesmith, were built, and they were skimpy and inadequate. Nonetheless Murray excelled and eventually received an annex used jointly by the Park District.

Land cleared of valuable housing next to the Ray elementary school was never used to build a replacement school. Instead many years later the school added a well-designed annex that permitted the original building, a gracious local landmark, to be preserved. While the physical condition of these schools benefited from community activism, overall the fact that neither the state nor the city would invest sufficiently in education undercut Hyde Park–Kenwood's long-term ability to retain middle-class families.

*

Sixty years after the creation of a racially balanced community in Hyde Park–Kenwood, the racial balance persists. The 2000 census showed the community as 46 percent black, 37 percent white, nearly 10 percent Asian, and 4 percent Hispanic, while the remaining 3 percent identify themselves as multiracial. This level of diversity would not be unusual in any big-city neighborhood undergoing racial change. Racial change usually transforms a community within a few years. But apart from a substantial increase in the Asian population and the appearance of a self-identified multiracial group, the racial balance in Hyde Park–Kenwood has not changed substantially since 1960.

Hyde Parkers made a huge effort to achieve a stable racial balance because they wanted to live in an integrated community. They took great pride in the social, cultural, and institutional assets of their community. When they felt these assets were threatened by racial change, they organized to protect them. At the same time their belief that community assets, including the lakefront, the parks, the housing stock, and the schools, should be shared with black families pushed them to break new ground.

When legally enforcible segregation ended, blacks began to move into Hyde Park–Kenwood. Community organizing around the preservation of community assets and the prospect of an integrated neighborhood persuaded people to stay. Critics argue that when urban renewal began, the true motives of the planners and their supporters were revealed. Buildings were torn down not because they were run down but because black people might live in them. Other pundits, recognizing the persistence of a substantial black population after urban renewal, assert that middle-class blacks and whites got together to drive out the poor.

It is impossible to judge how sincerely white Hyde Parkers welcomed black neighbors. It is equally impossible to determine how willing either black or white members of the middle class were to live with poorer people of either race. Regardless, the neighborhood achieved a lasting racial balance and continued to be economically diverse. If a substantial number of whites intended to keep out all but a handful of black people, they failed. If both black and white members of the middle class intended to keep out the poor, they too failed.

The community was also left with two parallel but deeply conflicting narratives to describe how urban renewal had changed it. The stories are often retold and have achieved a biblical simplicity in the moral choices described and the spareness of the narration. According to one version, Hyde Parkers, sheltering like medieval peasants under the lordship of the University of Chicago, drew up the drawbridge to a haven of middle-age comfort and security after admitting a few blacks, then heartlessly condemned the surrounding neighborhoods to decay, crime, arson, and abandonment. The comic take on this version is summarized in the Mike Nichols/Elaine May crack about Hyde Park, where "black and white are shoulder to shoulder against the poor." Nichols and May paid no heed to the amount of subsidized housing available in the community, if they knew about it.

The alternative story tells how a group of fair-minded citizens, many of them women, organized their neighbors to resist panic peddling and white flight. Bolstered by the University of Chicago, they built a diverse community that demonstrated how racial integration could enhance middle-class well-being. The shortcomings of the expert advice that the fair-minded citizens relied on tends to be left out of this version.

In the first rush of attention paid to the community because of Barack Obama, these two narratives, always so close to the surface in Hyde Park, did not emerge. Outsiders focused on the current diversity, still unusual, and did not ask for a history lesson. But this choice of narratives still divides older Hyde Parkers in camps reminiscent of the Sunni and Shiites. The religion uniting them is the importance of the moral instruction furnished by Hyde Park's experience; the bitter doctrinal dispute is over which narrative is THE TRUTH about that experience.

Hyde Park–Kenwood emerged in the 1950s and 1960s as the portion of two South Side neighborhoods where blacks now resided but whites remained. Since blacks now lived throughout the South Side, the defining element was that whites remained. The question of whether whites would have remained without urban renewal is hard to answer. There is no control group. They did not remain elsewhere.

Urban renewal could not have been conceived of as a possibility without its acceptance by probably the majority of residents concerned about the future of their community. Nor would it have become a reality without the prestige of the University of Chicago and the willingness of politicians to invest millions of tax dollars.

Churches, synagogues, and cultural, educational, and service organizations supported urban renewal and benefited from it, particularly through land grants. Many religious and cultural entities liked being part of an integrated community and felt that the racial balance enhanced their efforts. Even so, the reduction in density hampered these organizations over time. In contrast, many members of the business community who supported urban renewal soon felt betrayed by the extent of the demolition and displacement within commercial areas. Most of these businessmen were white, which should be remembered when assessing whether those who lost the most under urban renewal in Hyde Park were black.

The University of Chicago remained surrounded by a community of scholars. The neighborhood provided an urban setting for a major university and a place for all its undergraduates and many of its graduate students, faculty, and staff to live. It is difficult to quantify, but many people, black and white, live and have lived pleasant and satisfying lives in Hyde Park–Kenwood. Many, including some formidable critics of urban renewal, have found it so comfortable that they are disinclined to live anywhere else.

What happened in Hyde Park–Kenwood is interesting because of the racial segregation that still prevails in most of the United States, including Chicago. Hyde Park–Kenwood never became the much-replicated model of interracial living that many community residents had hoped to see. It may have been a successful experiment, but it was not a successful model. The key elements of community mobilization, an anchor institution of the university's importance, and local political will needed to be coupled with large amounts of public money. But public money would not have achieved a racially balanced community without the other elements.

This racially balanced community created opportunities for progressive black and white politicians that they would not otherwise have had. Hyde Park was already the local base of progressive politics. Idealists could be found on both sides of the urban renewal issue. Now, in a city with an increasing black population, there were affluent, well-educated black Hyde Parkers eager to tackle urban problems and reform city government. Many white Hyde Parkers were eager to work with them. Hyde Park had been a privileged enclave from its inception. It remained a privileged enclave, but its new diversity meant that the community's political independence was more important to Chicago and eventually to the entire country.

SIX
POLITICS GETS
A NEW FACE

Richard J. Daley served as mayor of Chicago from 1955 until 1976, when he died of a heart attack while in office. When first elected he had already served as chairman of the Cook County Democratic Organization. Cook County covers 1,635 square miles, includes 130 municipalities, and by 1960 had a population of more than 5 million. Holding both offices placed Daley in a position of extraordinary power, which he ruthlessly exploited. In particular, controlling hiring in both county and city governments provided him with a vast number of patronage jobs. During Daley's tenure in office, the overwhelming majority of the city's aldermen were his staunch supporters, eager to receive their share of available jobs, contracts, and other benefits.

In the same 1955 election, Leon Despres (pronounced Duh-pray), a Hyde Parker since the age of three, was elected alderman of the Fifth Ward, a position previously held by the noted reformers Charles Merriam, Paul Douglas, and Robert Merriam. The Fifth Ward included Hyde Park, which was well on its way to integration in 1955, and part of Woodlawn, an entirely black community. When Despres was elected the ward was 60 percent white and 40 percent black. He served in the City Council from 1955 to 1975, lasting in office nearly as long as Daley while becoming his most determined and celebrated opponent.

Until Barack Obama's race for the U.S. Senate, Chicagoans knew Leon Despres as the most famous politician from Hyde Park. Harold Washington, later Chicago's first black mayor, lived in the community, but to nearly everyone who knew him, Leon Despres was Hyde Park.

As he lived to be 101, retaining his faculties and his vivid memories of the neighborhood in earlier days, Despres became a walking history of the neighborhood. He loved to tell an audience, especially schoolchildren, about the days when you could buy a live chicken on Fifty-third Street. He knew the community well and declared in his old age, "I am still in love with Hyde Park and all Paul Cornell did to make it possible."

Despres attended both public and private schools in Hyde Park and spoke positively about all of them. After his father's early death, Despres was part of Rabbi Emil Hirsch's confirmation class at Sinai Congregation. Despres later believed this experience "helped to make up for the absence of a male figure." Rabbi Hirsch taught that as a religious principle, every human being was entitled to equal opportunity regardless of color. Just as he had inspired Julius Rosenwald to undertake philanthropy, including groundbreaking work on behalf of black Americans, Hirsch deeply influenced Despres. Thus Hirsch's teachings re-

Rabbi Emil G. Hirsch, a powerful voice for social justice, deeply influenced prominent Hyde Parkers. *(University of Chicago Library, Special Collections Research Center)*

mained alive in Chicago politics many years after his death in 1923.

After several years of study in Europe, Despres attended the University of Chicago and its law school. In 1932 he decided to get involved in "real" politics instead of the left-wing theory that had fascinated him. He attended a meeting of the Fifth Ward Democratic party, armed with a suitable letter of introduction to the ward committeeman. The committeeman's focus on patronage disgusted him. "What a ghastly aim of government, the plums of patronage! This was my last expedition to 'reality.'"

As a result, Despres joined the Socialist party immediately after the meeting. He was in good company at the time. As noted earlier, many Hyde Parkers, including Maynard Krueger, who was prominent in the national party, believed socialism would prevail.

Traveling in Mexico, Despres had the opportunity to meet Leon Trotsky, whom Joseph Stalin had forced out of Russia and into exile. Despres later recalled having a lengthy conversation with Trotsky and referred to him as the most impressive person he ever met. Characteristically, however, he offered no assessment of Trotsky's views on government or democracy.

Later Despres joined the Independent Voters of Illinois, a nonpartisan anti-Communist group affiliated with Americans for Democratic Action and devoted to supporting reformers. Twice he enthusiastically endorsed Robert Merriam for alderman. Despres later claimed that "In 1947 and 1951 'Merriam for Alderman' resounded like the tones of the University of Chicago carillon." Despres conceived of political merit as having the same impact on people as art or music—a creative response but one not shared by many.

When Merriam decided to run for mayor, a group of local activists asked Despres to run for alderman of the Fifth Ward in his stead. Despres writes that he was stunned to be asked to run because he believed his "record was too radical." It is not clear why Despres felt he was too radical for Hyde Park. His support for the labor movement was not more extreme than that of Paul Douglas, at that time a U.S. senator, or of Hyde Park rabbi Jacob Weinstein, a prominent labor activist. His comment betrays his need to be considered a radical.

Despres' immediate personal goal as an aldermanic candidate was to win more votes than the 650 Maynard Krueger had received as a Socialist candidate in 1935. As it turned out, the militant Marxist Krueger had been too radical for Hyde Park, but Despres was not. He won, and his victory became the community's consolation prize for Robert Merriam's loss in the mayoral election. Hyde Park could not select the mayor, but they could provide him with an exceptionally talented and forceful critic.

Leon Despres discusses a favorite topic, the history of the Hyde Park Co-operative Society, with a constituent. *(University of Chicago Library, Special Collections Research Center)*

The Fifth Ward initially elected Despres because he was running in support of Merriam, the reform candidate for mayor, a lifelong Hyde Parker, and his predecessor as alderman. Subsequently Despres' constituents reelected him because of his opposition to Mayor Richard J. Daley. For his part, Despres had a successful law practice and had no desire to augment his income through patronage. He was therefore financially free to be the independent representative his constituents wanted.

Despres saw Daley as a man driven by his need for power over the city government. He was a reformer, Despres said, but his reform was "always in the direction of increasing his power as mayor." Charles Merriam had also sought to increase the mayor's power in order to rein in unruly and easily corrupted aldermen. Of course he envisioned greater mayoral power in the hands of an enlightened progressive. Daley's tenure in office demonstrated that a more powerful mayor did not necessarily promote the kind of reform progressives like Merriam wanted. In fact it achieved the opposite goal. Meanwhile Daley reined in the aldermen very successfully, except for Alderman Despres.

Despres and Daley both loved Chicago but had little else in common. Despres was an attractive man, even elegant. Daley in 1955, according to his biographers Adam Cohen and Elizabeth Taylor, was a "short and pudgy man" who had "a face that drooped into a vast expanse of hanging flesh." Despres' manner was courtly, Daley's brusque. While Despres spoke eloquently, Daley's speeches were awkward and occasionally incomprehensible. Each man had a law degree—Despres' from the University of Chicago, Daley's from DePaul, earned at night. In their tastes and cultural interests, they were polar opposites.

Despres had strong intellectual and artistic interests that were central to his sense of himself. In his memoirs is a photograph of himself standing next to the left-wing French intellectual and Communist fellow traveler Jean-Paul Sartre. Despres and his wife had a deep and continuing interest in the visual arts and enjoyed collecting art. They purchased the work of black artists. They shared the Rosenwald Fund's intuition that understanding the artistic contributions of blacks broadened the cultural, social, and political acceptance of blacks as fellow citizens. They combined this insight with a sophisticated sensibility.

At times Despres' intellectual expertise served him well, as when he fought to prevent the City Council from ordering Wright Junior College to remove James Baldwin's *Another Country* from its required reading list. He begged the council not to make themselves a laughingstock in an attempt to lynch a book. He was fully aware of both the book's merit and the racist intent of the book banners.

At other times his need to be the most radical thinker in the room—and therefore in his mind the most moral—deepened his isolation even from people who shared many of his goals. He insisted, for example, on arguing that in a street gang there was something deeply valuable that needed to be preserved. When he made a comment like that, he was acting on his sense of himself as a public intellectual whose role was to formulate what should be the community's highest moral concerns. Unfortunately he valued his insights based on whether or not they pleased him intellectually and aesthetically, not whether they made any sense in the real world or were likely to advance a political cause.

His interest in research and in finding the right answer to meet people's needs was in the tradition established by Charles Merriam and carried on by Paul Douglas and Robert Merriam in their turns as alderman. Many have observed that same wonkish determination to find the right answer in Barack Obama. At any rate, Despres' willingness to investigate frequently enabled him to make such timely and appropriate suggestions that Mayor Daley quickly appropriated them. Examples would include an elevator safety ordinance and one restricting the use of lead-based paint. Both passed the City Council quickly once they had been reintroduced without Despres' name on them.

When Despres first joined the council he was greeted by Matthew Bieszczat, a hostile machine alderman who warned him against behaving like his predecessor Robert Merriam. Alderman Vito Marzullo called him names and threatened to beat him up. Marzullo, an Italian immigrant who did not complete elementary school, could not tolerate any hint of criticism of his beloved mayor and boss. Paul Douglas recounts similar experiences in his memoirs. But while Douglas overcame this hostility and arrived at a convivial relationship with his opponents, Despres never achieved that comfort level.

His experiences in isolation on the council shaped his public persona as an alderman and as a spokesman for the black community. To begin with, he hoped to work with black aldermen despite their affiliation with Daley. As he wrote, "Each of them knew much more about racial discrimination than I." But when he realized how financially dependent the black aldermen were on both Daley and William Dawson, he gave up.

Despres became the lone voice against racism in the Chicago City Council. When he arrived on the council, the black aldermen who served with him were unwilling to oppose Daley, even when he acted against the interests of the black community. Despres became the City Council spokesman for the black community, though he was white. He in fact represented a substantial number of black people because his ward was 40 percent black. But his evolution into what the *Negro Digest* called the "lone Negro spokesman" on the council was entirely unexpected.

Despres was not elected to serve as the voice of the black community; no one could have conceived of a white person in that role. This was true as early as 1915 when Oscar DePriest was elected as Chicago's first black alderman. He spoke out loudly and firmly on behalf of his community and was not afraid to offend whites. He was, in the language of the day, a "race man."

By 1955, however, there were no race men on the Chicago City Council. This reflected the extent of Daley's control and the level of obedience he expected. The Fifth Ward was the exception to that control. Despres' base of support in Hyde Park, his ability to earn a good living as a lawyer without relying on politically motivated referrals, and his personal indifference to patronage gave him the freedom to attack Mayor Daley, a privilege denied to the black aldermen of his day.

One man who might have been the council's missing race man in 1955 was Roy Washington, the father of Chicago's first black mayor. Washington, an able and independently minded lawyer, found his path to an aldermanic seat blocked by machine politics when he sought election to the City Council in 1947. His son, fourteen years younger than Despres, chose to enter politics via the state legislature rather than the City Council, deeply influenced by his father's disappointing experience. In time Barack Obama would choose a similar path to national politics through the state legislature, avoiding city government.

Earlier Robert Merriam had enjoyed the same support from an independently minded Hyde Park community that Despres now received, and they shared the same distaste for patronage. But while Merriam had progressive views on race relations and expressed concern for the black community on many occasions, he was never regarded as a spokesman for black Chicagoans. The roots of Despres' willingness to go so much further than Merriam ever did seem to lie in the uncompromising commitment to equality he learned from Rabbi Hirsch and his own need to visibly hold a radical moral position.

The first two black independent aldermen did not arrive on the council until 1963, when Despres had already served eight years. William Cousins, the black alderman Despres most admired, was not elected until 1967. These allies gave Despres colleagues but not enough support to win a contested vote in the City Council. Charles Chew, an independent black alderman elected in 1963 by middle-class black voters increasingly unhappy with Daley and his machine, teamed with Despres to introduce an open-housing ordinance to guarantee equal access for blacks. Mayor Daley's black supporters on the council led the counterattack. When the bill was defeated, Daley introduced his own open-housing ordinance, a watered-down effort designed to be toothless.

When Martin Luther King and his followers sought to march in Chicago, Mayor Daley fought them in court. He succeeded in getting an injunction imposing extensive restrictions on the planned marches. A City Council resolution was introduced praising Daley's actions. Only Despres voted against it. All seven black aldermen voted yes.

In time Daley accepted Despres' presence. In 1964, when some of Daley's lieutenants wanted to challenge Despres in the upcoming election, Daley told them to forget it and instructed the regular organization to work for Despres. It is not clear whether Daley did not wish to lose votes in the Fifth Ward or did not want to divert resources to a battle he might lose. Daley did not like dissent, but losing to Despres after a pitched battle would have been a major embarrassment. This did not mean that Daley had ceased to resent Despres; he continued to oppose him at every turn.

Despres' actions in the City Council were purely political theater because they were undertaken with no hope of prevailing or even influencing the outcome. In regard to matters where Despres did have direct access, he was often too isolated on the high ground to be effective.

In his memoirs, published late in his life, Despres recalls being opposed to Hyde Park's urban renewal plan because in his view it deprived the poor of public housing. He quotes with approval a visiting Englishman who called the plan "a cheat." He further suggests that he was nearly defeated for reelection as alderman because of his opposition to urban renewal. By contrast, in a 1962 essay on segregation that he published in *Chicago Scene*, he refers to Hyde Park–Kenwood, where urban renewal was in full swing, as an "island of hope" for blacks. What was Hyde Park—an "island of hope" or a "cheat"? Despres is of two minds.

He testified in support of the 1958 urban renewal ordinance. Before its passage, he worked hard to include a provision requiring scattered-site public housing, but he did not prevail. He wrote to Daley asking that the mayor support the inclusion of scattered-site public housing as a "moral token." In the most practical terms, it was Edwin Rothschild, not Leon Despres, who stepped forward to find sites for scattered-site public housing. Despres' leadership at the local level stumbled because he was bewitched by the moral campaign rather than aiming at fitting as many scattered-site public housing units as possible into the neighborhood.

Despres' record of dissent from Daley's policies on housing and employment is increasingly revered. Hyde Parkers, both black and white, were proud of his actions while he was in office. Today it is comforting when reading the history of the Daley years to hear Despres' voice raised time and again against racism, corruption, and indifference to the public good. But it is always a lone voice, crying out in the wilderness of total political isolation and impotence. Despres was respected while in office and even venerated in some circles. Yet he never won on a single issue while serving in City Council—unless his idea received Daley's approval and was reintroduced by another alderman.

Despite this experience, Despres' votes against Daley and his eloquent remarks on racial issues have come to provide a useful alternative narrative for many Chicagoans. Today his views on race are generally accepted, and his foes, chiefly Daley, have been fully discredited on this issue. Had I been there, a Chicagoan can tell him or herself, I would have sided with Despres.

Still, Despres' career constituted a clear warning to any aspiring young politician who aimed to exercise political power. The lesson was underlined by the fate of Abner Mikva. Like Obama, Mikva was a Hyde Parker and taught at the University of Chicago Law School. He served first in the Illinois House of Representatives and then in the U.S. House. He tackled hard, unpopular issues, becoming the bête noire of the National Rifle Association, which he dubbed the National Street Crime Lobby. His independence irritated Mayor Richard J. Daley, especially when in 1975 he endorsed Bill Singer, a reform candidate, who ran against Daley. Daley therefore conspired to move Hyde Park, Mikva's base, out of Mikva's congressional district into the neighboring First Congressional District, which was more than 90 percent black. To retain his seat in the U.S. House, Mikva would have had to challenge the well-liked black incumbent and Olympics hero Ralph Metcalfe.

Rather than wage a hopeless campaign, Mikva moved to Evanston, a northern suburb of Chicago. After losing one hard-fought race, he regained a seat in the U.S. House. He went on to a distinguished career as a federal appellate court judge and adviser to President Clinton. His career was, however, certainly diminished if not derailed by Daley's wrath.

If the message needed reinforcement there was also the example of the fate of the Fifth Ward itself. Throughout the aldermanic careers of both Merriams, Paul Douglas, and Leon Despres, the entire Hyde Park–Kenwood community lay within the boundaries of the Fifth Ward, giving Hyde Parkers an independent voice on the City Council. At the close of the 1970s, Larry Bloom was the Fifth Ward alderman. Bloom's independence annoyed Jane Byrne, one of the mayors who succeeded Richard J. Daley. In 1981 she arranged to split the traditional Fifth Ward in two, dividing Hyde Park–Kenwood between the Fourth and Fifth Wards, two newly drawn, predominantly black districts. Bloom won reelection anyway, receiving substantial support from black voters inspired in part by Harold Washington's endorsement of his candidacy. Despite his victory, Hyde Parkers still mourned the loss of their base.

Today Hyde Park is represented on the City Council by two black women, Toni Preckwinkle and Leslie Hairston. Preckwinkle of the Fourth Ward continues to oppose Mayor Richard M. Daley, the elder's son. Despres' voting record echoed Douglas's string of 1-49 votes while he served in the City Council. The

Abner Mikva, congressman, federal judge, and presidential adviser, is now Hyde Park's beloved and respected elder statesman.

high watermark of Douglas's tenure on the council was nine votes against a machine proposal. The pattern persists today. In 2007 Toni Preckwinkle, who at that time had the Obamas as constituents, reported proudly securing nine votes against the second Mayor Daley.

Thus from Charles Merriam's defeats as a reform candidate for mayor in 1911 and 1919 through to the present, Hyde Park aldermen have opposed a series of strong mayors. The exception came during the years that a Hyde Parker, Harold Washington, served as mayor.

*

Washington was born in Chicago in 1922 and had deep roots in the black church and in black South Side politics. His father,

Roy, a minister and the son of a minister, became a ward committeeman and a lawyer. Roy Washington struggled against the constraints on talented, aspiring blacks in politics and the legal profession. His son fought the same battles on a playing field that had expanded but was far from even.

Harold Washington's parents divorced, but he remained close to both and to a large circle of siblings and half-siblings. Throughout his life he was a warm and gregarious man, but he never acquired the habit of sharing his struggles. It is inconceivable to think of Washington writing as intimate a memoir as Obama's *Dreams from My Father*. Washington undoubtedly inherited dreams from his father and watched his father's deep disappointments, as when he lost the 1947 Third Ward aldermanic election. Washington and others believed that his father, an honest and well-respected man, had been badly treated by the Democratic party. Washington did not discuss this part of his life, but the lesson stayed with him.

At the segregated DuSable High School, Washington came under the influence of a remarkably talented teacher, Mary Herrick. Herrick had moved to Hyde Park to pursue a master's degree in political science at the University of Chicago. She was a gifted teacher who taught from 1916 to 1961 with interruptions for graduate study, research, and work on behalf of the teachers' union where she achieved a national role. She continued the tradition of tireless, selfless immersion in every aspect of social reform begun by Jane Addams and others of her generation. But her tactical skills as a politician far exceeded those of Addams.

Herrick brought her sense of urgency about equal opportunity and social justice into her classroom. She challenged the young men and women in her classes as students and citizens. Washington praised Herrick publicly throughout his career and said she stimulated more minds than any teacher he ever encountered. She also offered her friendship as a means of creating a bridge to the white world for young people confined within the Black Belt of Chicago. John Johnson, the founder and chief executive officer of Johnson Publishing, which publishes America's leading black periodicals, recalled later that she was the first white person ever to invite him into her home.

Washington dropped out of DuSable High School in his senior year. He served in the air force during World War II; he was denied a combat unit and instead built runways. After the war ended, he enrolled in Roosevelt University, recently launched in the heart of Chicago's downtown to educate working-class students of all races. Roosevelt was hastily organized and moved with no time to spare into a huge old hotel, a beautiful but neglected architectural masterpiece designed by Louis Sullivan. The school was committed to equal opportunity and benefited greatly from the numbers of talented black and Jewish students who were seeking an opportunity for higher eduction not available to them elsewhere. The student body was estimated to be one-eighth black and half Jewish.

Roosevelt was also able to hire a number of distinguished Jewish refugee scholars who, if they had not been exiled, would not have accepted appointments at a brand-new university. Other Chicagoans found new opportunities to teach at Roosevelt. St. Clair Drake, coauthor of *Black Metropolis*, began teaching there in 1946 and was given the chance to build one of the first black studies departments in the country,

In its early years Roosevelt had a supercharged political atmosphere. Many students were World War II veterans. The need for action and for a thorough overhaul of the political system were widely accepted. But every strategy was open to debate, every shade of left-wing opinion was represented. Many students looked for opportunities to confront discrimination in everyday life. Attempting to force local restaurant owners to seat racially mixed groups was a favorite grassroots activity. Students wanted to be able to eat while they talked for hours planning the postwar world, so their strategy served both personal and social-justice goals.

Washington moved confidently in this environment, which differed in important ways from the Black Belt politics of his youth. While Roosevelt students prized confrontation and dissent, Black Belt politics preferred loyalty and discretion. Nevertheless Washington was comfortable in a diverse, competitive urban student body. He was drawn to the power of language and ideas. His fellow students remember his able participation in debates on Shakespeare and political science. He does not have seem to have experienced the sense of dislocation and isolation that talented minority students often report after attending elite colleges. One measure of his ease with his fellow students came from his willingness, as a skilled painter, to paint friends' apartments free of charge. He had no money, they had no money. The paint job was something he could offer. Clearly he did not fear being defined as someone destined to do manual labor.

Washington emerged as a political leader at Roosevelt. In 1949 he was elected class president. During the same year he was the only black student among the group that went to meet with state legislators when they decided to investigate "radicals" at Roosevelt and the University of Chicago.

From the beginning Washington was a skilled parliamentarian and an excellent speaker. Beyond displaying these talents, he chose his political path at Roosevelt and never willingly deviated from it over the course of his life. He was a committed liberal and not a radical. He wanted equal opportunity under the law without compromise. At the same time he was a devoted centrist. He rejected "street action," though he never rejected the radicals themselves. He never attacked people for disagreeing with him. He attacked only if someone tried to block what he was trying to accomplish. Many years later he would receive valuable tactical support from left-wing Jews, often from Hyde Park, who were close kin to his fellow students at Roosevelt. He learned to work with them and benefit from their help without becoming involved in their own complex ideological wars.

At Northwestern Law School, Washington encountered an entirely different environment. He was the only black student in his class. Initially there were six female students, but only Dawn Clark Netsch, who became another formidable voice for reform in the Illinois legislature, remained to graduate with him. He was elected treasurer of the Northwestern branch of the American Bar Association, a testament to his easygoing manner and personal popularity. It had been only five years since the Chicago Bar Association had decided to admit black members.

After graduation Washington practiced law and joined Ralph Metcalfe's Third Ward organization. Metcalfe at this time was a loyal follower of Richard J. Daley. When Daley stripped Dawson of his patronage, it went to Ralph Metcalfe. Born in Georgia, Metcalfe had come to Chicago as a young man. He competed in the 1936 Berlin Olympics, winning a gold medal as a sprinter alongside his teammate Jesse Owens. He was first elected to the City Council in 1949 and quickly became Daley's favorite black protégé. Washington worked for the next ten years reviving and strengthening the Third Ward's Young Democrats organization. He learned what later came to be called community organizing, but from the beginning, unlike Barack Obama, his efforts were on behalf of the Democratic party. He was working for a political party that really had no place for him unless he was willing to surrender much of his independence.

The high ideals of Roosevelt's student body were hard to implement in Richard J. Daley's Chicago. The Democratic party rewarded Washington for his years of hard work with the opportunity to run for the Illinois House of Representatives. He was elected in 1965. The catch was that, having been elected with machine support, he had to pick his fights carefully and oppose the machine as infrequently as possible. Still, the Illinois legislature offered him more opportunities for independence than being an alderman would have allowed him. He was wise not to have tried to follow his father's example and seek election to the City Council. Although he chafed under the machine's yoke, in the legislature he was able to use his parliamentary skills, which would have been useless in City Council meetings. Greatly to Washington's credit, he compiled a strong record in the Illinois legislature while negotiating the shifting sands of Chicago's machine-driven politics.

Washington worked his way up to the State Senate and then to the U.S. House of Representatives. During this process he engaged in a bruising struggle with Richard J. Daley and the machine. His early independence diminished but did not disappear. His political life was a balancing act. He chose to vote present on those occasions when he could not vote against the machine. He was protected to some extent by Cecil Partee, president of the Illinois Senate and one of Daley's most important black allies. Partee intervened on at least two occasions to prevent Washington from being dropped from the Democratic party's slate. Nevertheless Partee's support for Washington, though consistent over the years, still depended on his own relationship with Daley, and that was always subject to change.

By 1975 white reformers and angry blacks were seeking a strategy to at least effectively attack Daley if not bring him down. The independent white alderman William Singer challenged Daley in the Democratic primary for mayor, and there was an earnest search for a black challenger.

Meanwhile big changes had occurred in the life of Ralph Metcalfe, Washington's political mentor. Shortly after his election to Congress in 1970 to replace the deceased Dawson, Metcalfe split with Daley, his political patron, over a series of incidents of police brutality. Daley turned on Metcalfe savagely, attempting to end his political career. Unlike the dispute with Dawson, Daley's fight with Metcalfe became a public battle. In 1976 when Daley refused to slate Metcalfe for his seat in Congress, Metcalfe ran as an independent Democrat and defeated Daley's chosen candidate handily. Metcalfe's survival made him a folk hero and showed that a black politician could win as an independent. Washington and others now urged Metcalfe to run for mayor. But Metcalfe declined and threw his support to Singer. Richard Newhouse, a black state senator from Hyde Park, made the run.

Newhouse was an elegant and well-educated man who had served in the army before graduating from the University of Chicago Law School. He became the first black to run for mayor of Chicago. Because he did not carry a single ward, his run might have looked symbolic. Singer did not carry a single black ward, so white liberals still appeared isolated on the lakefront. But adding Singer's votes to Newhouse's told a different story. White liberals plus disaffected, more affluent blacks produced a pool of potential reform voters that could challenge the mayor. The reformers could mount a real attack if blacks and whites could agree on a candidate.

In 1977 Harold Washington challenged Michael Bilandic, Chicago's barely competent mayor, in a special election held to fill the remainder of the late Richard J. Daley's term. Although Washington lost, the shape of his later winning coalition could be discerned. He won the endorsement of the Independent Voters of Illinois, the nonpartisan group based in Hyde Park. This did not bring him many votes outside Hyde Park, but it confirmed his credentials as a reformer. Unlike Newhouse two years before, he carried six wards that were black middle-class enclaves.

Meanwhile Jane Byrne, an Irish American who had served as Daley's commissioner of consumer affairs, in 1979 mounted an unlikely campaign for mayor. Bilandic squandered a substantial lead in the polls and through a series of comic misadventures with snow clearance handed her a surprise victory. Byrne's strongest supporters were middle-class black Chicagoans; over- all she received 59 percent of the black vote. If the election had been decided by whites only, she would have lost. Byrne had never been a candidate backed by the machine—because she had never been a candidate until this election. But her position outside the machine was enough to recommend her to voters looking for a change.

On the campaign trail Byrne had talked gamely about reducing corruption in city government. She had no strategy for accomplishing this and pursued an erratic course as mayor. Within a few months of taking office, she caved in to younger members of the machine serving on the City Council. She was capable of a compassionate gesture, for example when she moved into an apartment in a high-rise public housing develop- ment notable for its violence. But her gestures were not backed by concrete achievements. She could not manage the city with- out the support of the machine politicians she had previously attacked.

Washington's opportunity came in the 1983 Democratic mayoral primary. Jane Byrne was increasingly unpopular. Rich- ard M. Daley, Richard J.'s eldest son, was a popular state's attor- ney and an aspiring but unproven mayoral candidate. To Byrne's chagrin, she faced both Washington and Richard M. Daley in the Democratic primary.

Washington's victory in the primary and in the general elec- tion would require support from well-educated liberal whites. But he was not an entirely obvious choice for liberal white vot- ers. On the one hand, he was an eloquent speaker. A great reader and lover of the English language, he understood and delighted in the power of a well-chosen word. His silver tongue was in sharp contrast to Richard M. Daley, who mangled his incomplete sentences. On the other hand, Washington's always imperiled political situation had made him somewhat contemptuous of the rules that always seemed to favor the other guy. For several years in the early 1970s he had failed to file his income tax returns, even serving a brief jail sentence for the misdemeanor of failing to file on time.

Washington's victory was far from assured. Only a handful of black committeemen supported him. The only white committeeman who backed him was Alan Dobry, the Fifth Ward committeeman, who had devoted his life to opposing the machine. Dobry was, if possible, an even more unlikely Chicago ward committeeman than Douglas or Despres were unlikely Chicago aldermen. He had a Ph.D. in chemistry from the University of Chicago and a fine collection of modern art. He had supported Washington in previous campaigns for the Illinois legislature and the U.S. House of Representatives.

In the Democratic mayoral primary, Washington prevailed as Byrne and Daley split the white vote. Winning the Democratic nomination ordinarily signaled an easy victory in the general election, but Washington won a hard-fought general election by less than five percentage points. He faced determined white opposition from within the Democratic party. In an unprecedented move, Alderman Edward Vrdolyak, chairman of the Cook County Democratic party, supported the Republican candidate.

Ironically, Hyde Park provided both major-party mayoral candidates in the general election. Bernard Epton, a white liberal, was chosen as the Republican candidate to oppose Washington. Epton had represented Hyde Park in the Illinois House of Representatives. Although his legislative record was not that of a bigot, he mounted his campaign with the openly racist slogan "Epton Before It's Too Late."

Washington's coalition of blacks and reform-minded whites triumphed. The City Council was now no longer a rubber stamp. Reformers had long dreamed of the time when progressive measures would be debated on the council floor, and now they were. Yet they were often defeated. The racism that failed to defeat Washington in the election immediately confronted him in the City Council. Vrdolyak led a group of twenty-nine white aldermen committed to stopping his legislative agenda at every turn. Washington responded by vetoing the legislation passed by the Vrdolyak twenty-nine. They could not muster a thirtieth vote to overturn these vetoes from among the twenty-one black, white, and Hispanic aldermen who supported Washington.

Many Chicagoans grew impatient with the stalemate in city government. The *Chicago Tribune* fulminated that nothing was getting done in the City Council. The conduct of many aldermen was inept and embarrassing. Richard J. Daley had squelched any hint of leadership among the aldermen. The Chicago City Council had had almost no experience as a legislative body during his lengthy tenure, and this showed during their meetings. Washington was often blamed for the situation he inherited.

The black Jewish comedian Aaron Freeman wrote and performed a hugely popular satire about the City Council struggle called "Council Wars," after the hit movie *Star Wars*. Freeman mocked Washington's eloquence affectionately, calling him Harold SkyTalker. Hyde Parkers saw the council wars as a struggle between good and evil. They were proud that their alderman Larry Bloom, from the Fifth Ward, who was white, and Tim Evans, from the Fourth Ward, who was black, were staunch Washington supporters.

Meanwhile a number of Hyde Parkers, both black and white, played important roles in Washington's administration. Among the most talented were Elizabeth Hollander, who was white

Harold Washington, left, campaigning in Chicago, 1983. He excelled at public speaking and relished campaigning. *(Associated Press)*

and served as commissioner of planning, and Jackie Grimshaw, who was black and served as director of inter-governmental affairs.

In his second mayoral race Washington won a decisive victory over Vrdolyak, who ran as a Republican. Redistricting in 1986, ordered by a federal judge, had already brought additional Washington supporters into the City Council, increasing his supporters to twenty-five. After his second electoral victory some machine aldermen bowed to the inevitable and began supporting the mayor. As his second term began, Washington could rely on forty votes. It seemed that victory in the courts had been followed by victory at the polls. A more open and representative City Council appeared to be at hand.

Near the end of the first year of that second term, Washington suffered a fatal heart attack. He had just embarked on his agenda when he died. His accomplishments as mayor are difficult to evaluate. He survived repeated assaults from Vrdolyak's forces. His foes, like those of Despres, have been discredited, and their racism is an embarrassing memory. Vrdolyak's reputation is further tainted by his subsequent career, advising corrupt politicians and pleading guilty to criminal charges.

Washington was on the right side of history, but was he an effective mayor? He treated every area of the city as having an equal claim on city services. He was willing to consider people of every race, religion, and gender for employment at every level. At the same time his administration did not tackle school reform, public housing, and other core issues. Whether those initiatives were delayed by council wars or were beyond Washington's capability is an open question.

But Washington was clearly the last reform mayor to date. After two years of Eugene Sawyer, a black alderman who was elected mayor by the City Council, Richard M. Daley won the general election to succeed Washington. While Daley has modernized many aspects of city administration, he is not a reformer. His administration is opaque and autocratic, yet he has been reelected five times. Should he serve out his current term, in 2011 he will break his father's record as Chicago's longest-serving mayor.

The opportunity to elect a successor reform mayor faltered for lack of a strong candidate. When Washington died, Hyde Park could not field a viable reformer with the drawing power of Douglas, Merriam, or Washington himself. The neighborhood was represented by two ambitious aldermen—Tim Evans, who is black, and Larry Bloom, who is white. Both challenged Daley in his early years, but neither gained much traction.

Richard M. Daley had seemingly good reform credentials when he was elected in 1987. He had served as Cook County state's attorney, meaning that he was the chief public prosecutor for the huge county that includes Chicago. He was widely credited with having run an effective office, free of undue political influence. Recently police scandals have tarnished his image as a prosecutor, but at that time his years as state's attorney gave him solid government credentials.

Harold Washington left Barack Obama one major political legacy: he broke with Chicago's core tradition of ethnic leadership whereby a mayor from one ethnic group relies on the leaders of other ethnic groups to bring along their ethnic compatriots. Washington said his people included all three million Chicagoans. Obviously the Vrdolyak followers rejected his leadership. But a surprising number of Chicagoans who were not black were happy to belong to Harold Washington's people. Characteristically, a revealing moment in Washington's administration came not on a black holiday but on April 30, 1986, when he welcomed Polish Americans to city hall to celebrate Constitution Day. Polish Americans substantially outnumbered Irish Americans, making Chicago the second-largest Polish city in the world after Warsaw. But they had never achieved the political influence they sought. On this occasion Polish-American Chicagoans complimented Washington on including their people in substantial numbers at every level of city government. Washington responded with graceful remarks indicating that he actually understood what Constitution Day celebrates, mentioning Poland's Solidarity movement and extolling democracy.

Harold Washington's name is on Chicago's wonderful new public library, a suitable monument to a man who loved books.

The public park opposite his Hyde Park apartment is named
Harold Washington Park, which includes a playground called
Harold's Playlot. Washington felt comfortable in Hyde Park.
He had spent much time in the neighborhood during the years
when he lived in the neighboring community of Woodlawn. He
liked to walk and loved the lakefront. When he was elected to
the U.S. House of Representative he moved to Hyde Park and
during his tenure as mayor lived in the Hampton House apartment building on the site of Paul Cornell's hotel, overlooking a
park and the lake.

Washington enjoyed the park. According to local lore, he
was fond of watching the colorful parrots nesting in a tree opposite the windows in his apartment. The parrots, members of
a species not native to the area, might not have survived in Chicago. Hyde Parkers recall that Washington claimed the parrots'
presence or absence would predict his political fate and that he
often checked on them, looking down from his window into
their large nests.

Washington had always told friends that whatever he undertook, he would rather be reading a book. Late in the evening
he could often be found checking the shelves at Reid Michner's
used bookstore in Hyde Park, a favorite among local professors.
He also shopped at the Seminary Co-op. Today Barack Obama
is that store's most famous customer. Jack Cella, Seminary's
longtime manager, remembers meeting Washington for the first
time, years before he became mayor. During his regular visits
Washington impressed Cella with his invariably thorough book-
by-book review of his three favorite sections—Chicago, political
science, and African-American studies. As mayor he continued
to buy a lot of books, standing in line with a good sized stack
while his bodyguard stood by impassively. His official car would
be double-parked outside the store on University Avenue.
Washington's taste in books was scholarly; he read the major ac-

ademic works in his favorite disciplines as they were published. His presence occasionally caused a stir at the Seminary Co-op, where he was always ready to chat with staff or customers.

Hyde Parkers respected Washington and liked him. His life story, especially his early struggles and his commitment to reform and inclusion, was appealing. His love of books and often-expressed affection for Mary Herrick encouraged Hyde Parkers to claim him. He exemplified the well-educated, reform-minded leadership they found comfortable and sought in black as well as white leaders. Leon Despres called him the greatest mayor Chicago ever had. Now that decades have passed and reform in city government has been so effectively stymied, his early death is even more regretted.

*

Washington's career overlapped with those of two other talented politicians who shared many of his goals. In 1978 Carol Moseley Braun and Barbara Flynn Currie were first elected to the Illinois House of Representatives as Democrats from Hyde Park when the community was part of a three-member district. Their election predated Harold Washington's successful run for mayor by five years. When Braun and Currie joined Washington in the state legislature, the current of new, nontraditional leadership seemed to be running strong. Hyde Park's political representation was becoming more diverse.

These two women kept Hyde Park's inclusive reform agenda alive, first on the state and then briefly on the national level, while it languished in city government. Well educated and articulate, they were a remarkable pair who set one record after another, beginning with their election when for the first time two women were elected from one district to the Illinois House. Braun later became the first and still the only black woman elected to the

United States Senate. Currie, who is white, became the first
female majority leader in the Illinois House. Braun rose to the
heights of national influence but was soon sidelined by scandals.
Currie, by contrast, has remained in the House leadership while
avoiding scandal in a remarkably corrupt environment.

Hyde Park contributed in important ways to the launching
of both their careers, and both still live in the neighborhood.
Early on Currie and Braun were often regarded as the salt and
pepper of Hyde Park politics. They were both young, good-
looking, and articulate. But they were not interchangeable, and
their careers reveal deeply rooted differences. In particular their
relationship with the community and the role that Hyde Park
played in their careers was quite different.

Barbara Flynn Currie is the quintessential hometown girl
who has done well. She grew up in Hyde Park. Her father
taught social work at the University of Chicago while her
mother, a schoolteacher, was active in the League of Women
Voters. Currie attended St. Thomas the Apostle, a local Catholic
elementary school, and the University of Chicago Laboratory
High School. She dropped out of the University of Chicago
to marry but returned to complete a bachelor's and a master's
degree in political science. After beginning work on a doctorate, focusing on women's organizations, Currie abandoned her
research to run for office. Unlike many Hyde Parkers, she never
expresses regret about not finishing her dissertation.

Currie experienced the integration of the community as a
child and has always felt comfortable in and supported by the
interracial community that emerged. She loves the neighborhood and has expressed deep concern over its decline in numbers, especially of young families.

As the wife, now the widow, of a respected law professor
at the university, Currie has enjoyed a secure social position in
Hyde Park apart from her status as an elected official. Both she

Hyde Parkers parading down Fifty-third Street on the Fourth of July include Barbara Flynn Currie, right, dressed as Uncle Sam, Toni Preckwinkle as the Statue of Liberty, and Barack Obama in mufti. *(Toni Preckwinkle)*

and her husband had natural theatrical talent. Currie performs in local satirical revues with aplomb, quite willing to make affectionate fun of her community. Her husband appeared for decades in featured roles in local productions of Gilbert and Sullivan operettas. He often mocked pompous politicians, as when he played the role of Pooh-Bah in *The Mikado*.

Currie identifies her work as a young woman with the League of Women Voters as the best preparation she received for serving in office. That is exactly how Flora Cheney prepared to serve in the Illinois House in the 1920s and how Emily Taft Douglas prepared for the U.S. House of Representatives in the 1940s. Why was this so much more useful than the study of political science? "Because when we researched an issue, we eventually had to agree on something," says Currie. "We learned how to force a consensus."

Once elected, Currie looked to other women representatives as role models, including Republicans. She is a lifelong Democrat but believes that women have a special contribution to make to political life. Thus she is the direct if unconscious heir of earlier Hyde Parkers who looked to women to lead reform efforts.

Braun did not grow up in Hyde Park but in a segregated South Side neighborhood, similar to where Michelle Obama was raised. Her father was a Chicago police officer and her mother a medical technician. When her parents divorced, her grandmother stepped forward to care for her. Again like Michelle Obama, she excelled in school. After graduating from the University of Illinois, she attended the University of Chicago Law School. Unlike Mrs. Obama, however, she did not receive love and support from parents who were a united couple. Her father was prone to violence. Braun did not have a happy childhood, saying later she had to "grow up fast." After graduating from law school and going to work for the Illinois attorney general's office, she married a fellow student from law school, a white lawyer named Michael Braun. They had one son and were later amicably divorced.

Whereas Braun had always wanted to be a politician, Currie first entered politics in the spirit of "why not?" She specifically mentions her friend Michael Shakman's decision not to run for the legislature and his encouragement that she make the run as factors that help explain her willingness to enter the race. Shakman had already filed his famous suit against the Cook County Democratic Organization, challenging patronage, which has continued for decades.

The state legislature turned out to be a place where Currie could immerse herself in public policy work. She was never tempted by the City Council, where she would have earned more money and been able to forgo the tedious travel between

Springfield and Chicago. She has never run for any elected office besides state representative.

Braun also thrived in Springfield. She showed impressive leadership skills and tackled big issues. For example, in 1984 she introduced a proposed moratorium on the death penalty. She also spearheaded litigation against the State of Illinois and her own party that led to increased black and Hispanic representation in the legislature.

Even in their first terms in office, Currie and Braun received very different kinds of support from Hyde Park's political community. Currie got political support; her emotional support came from her husband, family, and friends. She does recall dogged pressure from Lois Dobry, a feisty independent Democratic organizer, to speak up for herself. "Eventually Lois stopped applying a hat pin in the neighborhood of my ribs, so I assume I improved," Currie recalls.

For many years Currie's office staff consisted of one person, a brilliant, mercurial gay political activist called Forbes Shephard. He was always willing to put himself in harm's way to prevent election fraud. Election day has not really started, his friends would say, until Forbes has been kicked out of a precinct. Apart from his political work, Shephard was a fine pianist. But the political world was not yet ready for him, and Currie's home office became his haven.

Braun relied on strong and intelligent women to run her office. Unfortunately she needed endless emotional support, and one by one they quit, too drained to continue. When she later got the love she needed from weaker, less reliable people, it hurt her and her career.

Braun was more ambitious than Currie. She ran for and was elected Cook County Recorder of Deeds. Many Hyde Parkers were stunned that a brilliant debater and political analyst would wish to preside over such a dull, cumbersome bureaucracy.

Hyde Park, which considered itself Braun's home base, began to be puzzled by her decisions and miffed by her occasionally imperious behavior.

In 1991 Alan Dixon, the veteran Illinois Democrat who was serving as U.S. senator, voted to confirm Clarence Thomas as a Supreme Court justice. Women everywhere wanted to punish him. Braun declared her intention to oppose Dixon, and in 1992 she ran against him in the Democratic primary. When she began her campaign she had little money, and few pundits thought she had a chance. She had, however, fierce and skilled support from local Democratic women, including former staffers from her days in the legislature.

In the primary Braun defeated Dixon and another well-funded white male opponent, receiving 26 percent of the white votes. She went on to defeat a veteran Republican politician, Richard Williamson, in the general election and became the first black woman in the U.S. Senate. During the primary her campaign was transformed from a local battle into a national crusade. Her fund-raising took off, and much of the money came from outside Illinois.

Braun was photogenic, had a wonderful smile, and was quotable. Like the Merriams, Despres, and Douglas, she was a Hyde Park politician the media loved. She proved that Illinois, despite the political power of the conservative, largely white, southern portion of the state, could unite behind an urban black candidate. Her leadership abilities, skills in debate, and strong personality promised a notable career in the U.S. Senate. But the factors that would sabotage her career were evident even as America celebrated the Year of the Woman with Carol Moseley Braun as the star.

Braun's transition from Cook County to the U.S. Senate was abrupt. She never understood that she had to change her fiscal habits entirely in order to stay in the Senate. She continued to

Like Barack Obama, Carol Moseley Braun's intellectual gifts and compelling personal story help fuel a meteoric rise. She was undone by personal choices. *(Getty Images)*

raise and spend money in a manner that would not have raised eyebrows in Cook County but was not acceptable in national politics, where both the expectations and the level of scrutiny are higher. She publicly reveled in her new affluence. After her famous boast that her successful fund-raising meant "God willing, I will never go hungry again," the press said she sounded like Scarlett O'Hara. Older Chicagoans thought it sounded more like William Dawson, the long-term Chicago congressman who had been famously devoted to his own financial preservation. But he would never have been foolish enough to say it to the press.

Braun's involvement with Kgosie Matthews, a South African who became her campaign manager and fiancé, was a personal and professional disaster. Again her expectations were shaped by political life in Cook County. The local press has shied away from the sex life of politicians in Chicago unless a scandal is forced into the open by a rival candidate.

When Braun described Kgosie Matthews as her knight in shining armor, her supporters cringed. When he was repeatedly accused of sexually harassing her staff, the accusations made her zealous attack on Clarence Thomas look hypocritical. The unfavorable publicity hurt her, but the consequences went deeper than bad press. Braun was surrounded by well-wishers, some of whom could have helped her greatly. Instead of reaching out, she isolated herself and relied on the advice of an inexperienced and incompetent man who devoted himself to driving away the rest of her staff.

Braun had her finest moment in the Senate when she led the charge against the renewal of a design patent that included the Confederate flag. She turned the occasion into a frank discussion of racism, perhaps the last national discussion of the issue until Obama made his groundbreaking speech on the subject. Braun brought her colleagues with her, showing a brand of leadership she rarely displayed in the Senate.

Her relationship with Kgosie Matthews, who had worked as a lobbyist for Nigeria, resulted in an embarrassing visit to that country, where she heaped praise on the ruthless dictator Sani Abacha. The fees she received from Smith-Glaxo-Kline, the British drug company, resulted in her casting embarrassing votes against closing a loophole in the tax code that benefited that company.

Braun was defeated in her second race for the Senate. Currie says Braun could have won but "her heart was not in it." Sue Purrington, a former staffer and close friend, says "her head wasn't in it." In 1999 President Clinton appointed her U.S. ambassador to New Zealand, and she served until 2001. Her 2004 campaign for the U.S. presidency attracted little support but did restore some of the credibility and respect she had enjoyed earlier.

Today, at the age of sixty-two, Braun is invisible in Hyde Park. She busies herself promoting natural foods. By contrast,

Abner Mikva, who is in his eighties, still serves as chairman of nearly every commission investigating a local scandal and takes an active role in promoting younger politicians he admires.

Currie continues to serve in the Illinois state legislature. She champions good government, social welfare, and women's issues. The political pedigree of her agenda can be traced straight back to Flora Cheney and the progressives. In 1997 she became the first female majority leader in the Illinois House of Representatives. She has maintained an irreproachable reputation for integrity in the wildly corrupt world of Illinois politics. In 2008 the speaker of the house chose her to preside over the committee that impeached then Governor Rod Blagojevich.

Both Braun and Currie drew strong support from both blacks and whites, providing a foretaste of Obama's cross-racial appeal. Currie has been repeatedly reelected from a district with a black majority. Various black challengers have made no inroads on her popularity.

When Braun ran for the Senate she carefully projected her personal story, relying on her experiences as a mother and her early struggles to connect with white voters, especially women. Again her success in convincing white voters that they had a lot in common with her paved the way for Obama.

Currie has continued to insist on the importance of women's perspectives in politics, but she has not made much political use of her personal story. She is a polished public performer who disdains tugging at people's heartstrings. The public never heard, for example, about her husband's long battle with the illness that eventually killed him. Instead Currie's popularity with both the black and the white middle class reflects their preference for an intelligent, well-educated, rather classy reformer, reminiscent in some ways of Leon Despres.

Carol Moseley Braun's missteps in the U.S. Senate have largely obliterated the memory of the promise she once showed.

In Hyde Park, people remember her talents and shake their heads over her political fate. Hyde Parkers had always been willing to show her much the same love they showered on Barack Obama. She was the gifted, young black politician of her generation, at ease both in black neighborhoods and in white academic circles. But from the start Braun did not find in Hyde Park the affection, support, or income she sought. The neighborhood helped her start her career but could not help her sustain her political viability. Hyde Parkers wound up watching her crash like spectators at the scene of a car wreck.

*

Like his father, the current mayor of Chicago, Richard M. Daley, has been a strong leader. The second Mayor Daley has not lost more votes in the Chicago City Council than his father did. Chicago city government is not open, transparent, or accountable. Each year when Chicago's fifty aldermen arrive for the city's budget hearings, they receive thick briefing books that have no numbers in them.

As Fourth Ward alderman Toni Preckwinkle observes, "The mayor mistakes dissent for treason." Disagreement is not allowed, discussion is not encouraged. People who differ publicly with the mayor disappear from his administration and, if the mayor can arrange it, from public life. This type of power was once common in large cities run by political machines. In the twenty-first century, Richard M. Daley alone exercises that level of authority. Apparently most Chicagoans are happy to see him hold this degree of power. The last time he ran for reelection he received more than 80 percent of the vote.

In the past Hyde Park's relationship with machine mayors was straightforward: Hyde Parkers opposed the mayor, and the mayor won. Hyde Park's relationship with this mayor is more complicated. Hyde Parkers have worked hard to deprive the mayor of patronage, continuing their traditional opposition to machine politics. At the same time Hyde Park has provided the mayor with key administrators and effective strategies on important issues, including public education.

In theory Richard M. Daley has had to run the city without an important weapon in his arsenal. By law the younger Mayor Daley has not been able to use large-scale political patronage hiring to reward supporters. Patronage jobs provided the lifeblood of his father's machine. It was a Hyde Park attorney, Michael Shakman, whose quest to end patronage, begun with a lawsuit filed in 1969, was ultimately successful—at least on paper.

In 1969 Shakman ran as an independent candidate to be a delegate to the 1970 Democratic National Convention. In those days Mayor Richard J. Daley, in his role as chairman of the Cook County Democratic Organization, chose Chicago's delegation. Shakman filed suit against the organization, arguing that the patronage system, under which organization loyalists received government jobs in return for political work, placed candidates like himself, who were not sponsored by the organization, at an illegal and unconstitutional disadvantage.

In 1972 Shakman and the Cook County Democratic Organization entered into a negotiated settlement that forbade firing, demotion, and transfer as political punishment. Subsequently a court order in 1983 ended any consideration of political factors in Cook County government hiring or firing, except in the case of a few highly placed policy positions. The Shakman Decrees, as the rulings came to be known, are in full force today in numerous jurisdictions, including the City of Chicago.

So Hyde Park reformers, through the courts, achieved the end of apolitical hiring they had sought unsuccessfully at the polls. The victory has proved hollow. Mayor Richard M. Daley has fewer jobs at his disposal than his father did because the overall size of city government has shrunk, but political hiring continues, supplemented by granting major contracts for work once done by city employees to politically favored firms. Patronage has evolved but has not disappeared. The same courts that entered the Shakman Decrees have investigated and confirmed the extent to which the city has ignored the rules.

The federal court appointed a monitor to oversee city hiring practices, but the monitor's reports have not been encouraging. In 2007 Shakman responded to the monitor's report by saying, "In my view they're getting an F from the monitor. This is not a city that wants to set things straight." Shakman's suit was a civil matter. Criminal charges have also been filed, underlining the fact that improper political hiring has continued. As recently as 2005, Robert Sorich, Richard M. Daley's chief of patronage, went to prison for running a classic city-jobs-for-sale scheme. He was convicted of mail fraud, but the basis for prosecution was traditional patronage.

Whatever public outrage exists over the failure to end patronage, it is not translated into votes. The black community has been the last holdout against Richard M. Daley's popularity. He received the majority of the black vote for the first time only in 2003. A series of black candidates of diminishing stature has run against him. The mayor has been widely praised for moving beyond Chicago's divisive tradition of racial politics. Does he deserve this praise?

When he was first elected mayor, Daley faced two successive black candidates, Eugene Sawyer and Tim Evans. Neither Evans nor Sawyer matched the caliber of Harold Washington as a candidate. In the next election, two years later, Daley seemed to face a much more challenging black candidate in the Democratic primary. Danny Davis, a former alderman who had become a Cook County commissioner, looked strong. He had been a loyal supporter of Harold Washington in the City Coun-

The author with Mayor Richard M. Daley and kids in costume, launching the city's summer festivals program in the late 1980s.

cil and was untainted by service to the first Mayor Daley. He had demonstrated he could move beyond the City Council by getting elected to the Cook County Board of Commissioners. Like Washington, Davis was well educated and articulate. He had never indulged in the kind of rhetoric that repelled liberal white voters. So he seemed guaranteed to appeal to black voters and likely to attract a respectable portion of the white electorate.

Instead Davis received only 30 percent of the vote. The percentage is less striking than the significant decline in the number of voters. What had happened to the black vote? Whatever the reason, black voter participation continued to decline. In 1995 Joe Gardner, a pleasant but uncharismatic black politician, received fewer votes than Davis had. Again, fewer blacks voted overall.

In 1999 when black congressman Bobby Rush ran against Daley, black voter participation appeared to rise. Daley defeated Rush with 68.9 percent of the vote but did not get a majority of the black vote citywide.

Running so unsuccessfully against Daley did not hurt the careers of either Davis or Rush. In 1997 Davis went on to be elected to the U.S. House of Representatives. In 2000 Rush handily defeated Barack Obama to retain his seat in Congress.

In 2003 Daley finally received a majority of the black vote. His overall vote total rose to 71.5 percent and then to 80.2 percent in 2007. His opponent in 2003 was a nonentity named John Jakes; in 2007 it was Dorothy Brown, an unpleasantly egotistical county official.

These figures indicate Daley's overwhelming popularity. But focusing just on Hyde Park, divided between the city's Fourth and Fifth Wards, tells a different story. In Daley's early years, Hyde Park was far from receptive to him. Even Joe Gardner, a well intentioned but uninspiring candidate, won more than twice as many votes as Daley received in both the Fourth and Fifth Wards. Again, the vote total for Bobby Rush in the 1999 mayoral race was surprisingly high. White Hyde Parkers generally do not care for Rush. At the same time some middle-class blacks resent his exclusionary rhetoric and his decision in 1992 to run against the well-respected longtime black congressman Charles Hayes. Still, in 1999 Rush beat Daley in both wards. That Rush carried these wards has to be interpreted as a protest against Daley since Rush himself had little appeal for Hyde Park voters.

Apart from skepticism in Hyde Park and parts of the black community, Daley has scored crushing victories in the city. How has he retained such a firm hold over city government? There are many partial answers. The mayor is clearly motivated by a great love of his city, and the extent of that commitment inspires respect. He shrewdly understands and responds to many of the public's concerns. He speaks without eloquence but with passion.

Richard M. Daley's administration has been made more palatable by a strategy he learned from Washington. From the beginning of his first term in office, Daley placed blacks and Hispanics in influential positions. His father used blacks only to care for the concerns of other blacks. In contrast, Richard M. Daley is as inclusive as Washington was. For example, he is unexpectedly effective as a spokesman for gay rights. He simply asks why anyone would discriminate against "your neighbor, your cousin, or your brother."

Thus Daley has been willing to hire blacks, women, and gays, and place them in positions of authority. But only on his terms. Many competent administrators have broken with him because at some point in their career they disagreed with the mayor. Because Daley cannot accept criticism or disagreement, that ends the relationship. Two of his most highly regarded appointments, Valerie Jarrett and Arne Duncan, his popular education chief, proved to be unfailingly loyal to him and never publicly criticized the mayor. Both were and remain steadfastly silent about their Chicago boss. They have now transitioned to the Obama administration without ever damaging their relationship with Daley.

Daley turned again and again to Valerie Bowman Jarrett, a black woman who is also a longtime Hyde Parker. Jarrett grew up partly in Hyde Park and attended the University of Chicago Laboratory Schools, though she graduated from an eastern boarding school. She lived in Hyde Park as an adult and sent her daughter to the Laboratory Schools.

Jarrett comes from a family of extraordinary achievers whose careers have been intimately connected with Hyde Park for at least three generations. In 1888 her great grandfather, Robert Robinson Taylor, was the first black student at the Massachusetts Institute of Technology. He had a distinguished career as an architect, primarily at the Tuskegee Institute where he built many notable buildings. Taylor struggled to bring the high standards of his MIT classes to Tuskegee and to open the eyes of young black students to the merits of careers in engineering and architecture.

Taylor's son, Robert Rochon Taylor, moved to Chicago. Julius Rosenwald, the wealthy philanthropist who lived in Hyde Park and had supported Tuskegee, hired the younger Robert Taylor to manage the Michigan Boulevard Garden Apartments, The Rosenwald. Based on his work there, Taylor was asked to serve on the board of the Chicago Housing Authority (CHA), the agency governing all of Chicago's public housing built and funded by the government. He eventually became the first black chairman of the CHA board.

Robert Rochon Taylor's memory was honored by the CHA, which named the huge Robert R. Taylor homes public housing development for him. This development deteriorated dreadfully and became a byword for crime and poverty. His daughter's and granddaughter's careers in public service are a better memorial.

Taylor's daughter Barbara Taylor Bowman, a longtime Hyde Park resident, became a leading advocate for and expert in early childhood education. She collaborated closely with Maria Piers, a refugee Jewish expert on child development, who also lived in Hyde Park, to found the Erikson Institute, now a major academic presence in this field. The Institute was launched in a few rooms in the Hyde Park Bank Building. Piers said later that it could have been started only in Hyde Park. Irving B. Harris, a contemporary successor to Julius Rosenwald as an innovative philanthropist, funded the enterprise.

Valerie Bowman Jarrett has brought a notable tradition of public service and quiet influence to new heights.

Barbara Bowman married a distinguished black doctor, and Valerie Bowman Jarrett is their only child. Jarrett entered Chicago politics as a member of the Washington administration. After his death, she joined the Richard M. Daley administration as the mayor's deputy chief of staff, as commissioner of the Department of Planning, and later as chairman of the board of the Chicago Transit Authority. Jarrett and Daley's relationship has remained intact. After she left the city administration to work for the Habitat Company, a politically connected real estate firm, she continued to receive high-profile assignments including the Chicago Olympics Committee, a particular pet project of the mayor's.

In 1991 Jarrett hired a young Michelle Robinson, who was engaged to Barack Obama, away from a Loop law firm to work for her in the Daley administration. They developed a close friendship, and Jarrett took the young couple under her wing.

Jarrett has always moved through Chicago politics with the assurance provided by her family background and her own professional qualifications. Her personal style has been that of her family. She never considered running for office, though she has assisted those who did. She valued affluence but never stooped to corruption. She expected to collaborate on projects at the highest level as an equal partner. She always placed the opportunity to have direct real influence on results above what other people might think of her. During a Hyde Park dispute over a community garden, Jarrett was annoyed that her opponents harassed her young daughter. If she has ever cared about harassment directed at her, she has never allowed that concern to show in public.

Jarrett could have broken with the mayor but has chosen not to, exerting formidable self-control. Her poker face does not crack in public. Her commitment has given the mayor a continuing connection with Chicago's Hyde Park–based black elite. Her loyalty to Daley presaged her near-legendary loyalty to Obama.

Daley's decision early in his career as mayor to take over the public schools was extremely popular and earned him great respect. Chicagoans value his willingness to tackle this difficult problem because almost everyone worries about the state of the schools. During the current mayor's childhood, Chicago had a comprehensive system of Catholic schools that rivaled the public schools in size. While the Catholic schools charged tuition, in those days it was low enough to allow access to working-class families. The Catholic school system has now shrunk drastically, increasing the demand for good public education.

Chicagoans understand that well-financed and well-functioning school systems have greatly benefited the suburbs and enticed families the city needs to retain. City school financing meanwhile has not increased. According to the state constitution, Illinois is supposed to provide half the cost of local public education, but the state fails to pay its share. The mayor has not been willing to put substantial city money into the schools. He has, however, been willing to put his reputation on the line and has put substantial direct pressure on the school administration to produce better results. He has made it clear that better results mean higher test scores for all students and that the schools must serve more middle-class families who do not wish to pay private-school tuition.

Arne Duncan, a lifelong Hyde Parker, was a huge asset to the Daley administration during his tenure as chief executive officer of the Chicago Public Schools. Like Valerie Jarrett, he moves through Chicago politics with patrician assurance. No hint of scandal has ever been attached to his name, in contrast to many other high-ranking Daley officials.

Jarrett and Duncan provided Hyde Parkers and other progressively minded Chicagoans with the reassurance that, however sordid city politics might be, Daley's administration was doing some things right. A level of comfort has thus legitimated passive acceptance of Daley's continuing control. At times, as scandals mounted, this justification wore thin. But this strategy received a huge retroactive boost when both Jarrett and Duncan joined the Obama administration, unscathed by any battles with Daley.

SEVEN
PURSUING GOOD
PUBLIC EDUCATION

Hyde Parkers have long tried to improve the quality of the Chicago public schools. Armed with high standards, they have brought the same tenacity and inclusive vision to public education that they have devoted to progressive politics. The University of Chicago has repeatedly launched ambitious plans to reshape public education that have often been smashed by political reality. Reformers have seen tremendous opportunities to serve children throughout the city wasted because of corruption and racism. Their efforts in this field provide a case study of their effectiveness in the arena of public policy generally. The historical record merits attention if only because a series of Hyde Parkers, including Arne Duncan, who currently serves as secretary of education, have had influential roles in public education.

This *Chicago Tribune* cartoon shows William Rainey Harper chasing after President Theodore Roosevelt as a speaker for his popular lectures program. Harper's tireless pursuit of his goals was as notorious in his day as Eleanor Roosevelt's in hers. (*University of Chicago Library, Special Collections Research Center*)

William Rainey Harper, the first president of the University of Chicago, had strong ties to the Chautauqua, the popular late-nineteenth-century adult education movement that combined showmanship with religious zeal to bring culture to the masses. His plans for the new University of Chicago included a large extension program. Harper's broad vision reverberates in current debates over educational reform. He cared about the quality of primary and secondary education in general, not just for those students bound for the University of Chicago or a comparable institution. He understood that everyone's education mattered.

In 1896 John Dewey, a professor at the University of Chicago and one of America's most famous philosophers, founded the University of Chicago's Laboratory Schools. The schools extended from nursery school through high school. As the name openly proclaimed, the schools were intended to serve as a laboratory where Dewey's idea about education could be tested with children. Dewey believed that children's learning should be rooted in their experience. He thought they should discover much of what they learned through purposeful activity, not from textbooks. In the early years of the Lab Schools, Dewey's emphasis on "learning by doing" was derided as pure play, and critics cited the school as an example of unrealistic intellectuals engaged in an irresponsible experiment.

Dewey's vision for the schools—he intended to transform public education—was never fulfilled. Instead he founded what became an expensive, well-regarded private school. Over the years influential educational ideas were introduced at the Lab Schools. Some of these ideas included the introduction of science and foreign language at an early age. Dewey passionately believed in the power of education to produce good citizens and the need for equal opportunity in a democracy. These goals have inspired many efforts to improve education and still resonate with Hyde Parkers, among others.

At the turn of the twentieth century, two very different attempts were made to bring ideas developed at the University of Chicago to bear on the Chicago public schools. Neither was successful, but both reveal fundamental issues that still confront those who seek to improve public education.

Harper tried first. He joined the Chicago Board of Education in 1896, as soon after his arrival as he qualified for membership under the residency requirement. At first he sought to influence the caliber of education in the city schools primarily by educating teachers. Harper did not believe that providing basic teacher training and the highest level of research at differ-

John Dewey's work created a direct connection between the intellectual elite and the drive to improve public education that is missing today. *(New York Public Library)*

ent branches of the University of Chicago created any conflicts or required any lowering of standards.

In time he sought more direct input into the administration of the schools. In 1897 he was delighted to serve as chairman of a commission appointed by the mayor to study the schools and make recommendations. Harper devoted enormous energy to the commission's work and made it a high priority, against the advice of some university trustees. He directed extensive research into the condition of the public schools and recruited other university presidents to endorse his recommendations.

The plan that emerged from this work, popularly known as the Harper Report, sought a smaller board of education, which in fact Chicago has today. Harper wanted to put the board under the direct control of professional educators and administrators. He aimed at limiting the influence of Chicago politicians, especially those representing the poorly educated immigrant communities. He feared that corrupt Chicago aldermen would pressure board members to serve their personal and political interests. At the same time he thought a smaller, better-educated, and more affluent board would understand what children from poor neighborhoods needed without any representation from those communities.

Harper's methods and his agenda are strongly reminiscent of Charles Merriam's. Both men said they wanted to end political influence, whether in public education or public transportation. They meant they wanted to end the influence of politicians they considered corrupt and ignorant. Both men were perfectly willing to achieve their ends through political means. They supported changes in governance that they believed would strengthen progressive politicians and administrators who agreed with them. But the strong centralized authority they advocated, whether exercised by the mayor or a small school board acting in the mayor's name, did not advance the cause of reform when the strong mayor was not a reformer.

The Harper Report was clear about the challenges the authors felt public education in Chicago faced. They were concerned about the high proportion of children who came "from families to whom English is barely known" and whose home life was "utterly opposed to the requirements of American citizenship."

Harper wanted higher educational qualifications for teachers. At the time most public school teachers were women, and many of them who taught elementary school had not even completed high school. They were poorly paid and struggling to support themselves and family members. Men were paid more than women. Harper was willing to continue to offer higher pay to men in order to attract more men to teaching, a proposal that alienated women teachers.

At this time members of the Chicago Board of Education regularly made decisions about the hiring and firing of teachers, and the choice of textbooks and curriculum. Harper wanted a superintendent with greatly increased powers who could make all those decisions and control all educational issues. The venal motives that Harper suspected did indeed often influence board members' actions. To make matters worse, the board members disagreed with one another and sometimes issued conflicting orders.

Harper further suggested that the superintendent be assisted by a business manager, freeing him to focus on educational issues. That suggestion has a very modern ring. Interestingly, a later Harper Report recommended the opening of school buildings for community use on terms that sound very much like the current emphasis on extending the school day and providing more social services at schools.

Determined opposition to Harper's plans came from several quarters. Local politicians wanted a hand in the hiring and firing of teachers, either by serving on the board or by controlling board members. In their eyes teachers were patronage workers, no different from other city employees. Politicians also wanted a voice in school contracts in order to collect a share of the funds and favor their supporters.

Even the teachers who understood the downside of patronage hiring in the schools did not rally to Harper's cause. Margaret Haley, a leader of the Chicago Federation of Teachers, feared the concentration of power in the superintendent. She pointedly remarked that only Jesus Christ could be trusted to exercise as much authority as Harper planned to give the superintendent.

Harper and other reformers failed to persuade either the leadership or the rank-and-file teachers that a strong, professional superintendent, backed by a small school board drawn from the local elite, would treat them fairly and raise their pay without the protection of a union. This failure had consequences that are still felt today. After bruising and lengthy battles lasting into the 1920s, the teachers won the right to unionize. In 1937 four separate labor organizations merged to form the Chicago Teachers Union. Prominent reformers, including Paul Douglas and some University of Chicago faculty, strongly supported the new union. It succeeded in ending political control over promotions, raising pay and improving working conditions.

Today the pendulum has swung again, and many reformers maintain that union rules prevent innovation. The University of Chicago has strongly backed charter schools, which are not required to hire union members or abide by the union contract. Thus Harper's successors attempt to convince current teachers that a strong professional superintendent, backed by a small school board drawn from the city's elite, will treat them fairly without the protection of a union contract. As this is exactly the argument that Harper made to teachers about a century ago, it will be fascinating to see if they are more successful than he was.

Many reformers hailed the Harper Report, as did members of the business community. Proposals based on Harper's plans were repeatedly introduced in the state legislature, but failed. Some of the reformers' goals, however, were met. Educational requirements for teachers were raised. The reformers wanted more record keeping in the schools and much more emphasis on the accurate assessment of student achievement. With the help of academics who wanted to study schools, they fulfilled their goal, and research into student and school performance flourished. This was and is the area where academic influence is strongest. But comprehensive reform imposed from outside the school system clearly failed.

*

Ella Flagg Young, who served as superintendent of the Chicago public schools from 1909 to 1915, made a very different attempt to bring ideas from the University of Chicago into public school classrooms. She mounted her campaign from within. Her extraordinary leadership skills made her the first woman to serve as superintendent of a large urban school system. She was deeply influenced by her work with Dewey, first as his student and then as a colleague. What she learned at the University of Chicago was at the heart of her work as superintendent.

Young began teaching in the public schools in 1862 and struggled to make her lessons relevant to her immigrant students. She left teaching when she married, but having been widowed, without children, she returned to the classroom. Left with no close relatives, she concentrated her life on improving teaching and learning in the public schools. Eventually she sought a leadership role. From the beginning of her career in administration, she reached farther than most women.

Interestingly, when Young sought to become a principal in 1879, women were not required to take a principal's exam as men were. The exam was probably considered unnecessary for women because they were allowed to be principals of only the smallest elementary schools. When Young insisted on taking the principal's exam anyway, she passed and was assigned to a very large elementary school. With class sizes upward of eighty, teaching was a challenging occupation. The most remarkable feature of her career was the deep connection she made with teachers. It survived as she rose through the ranks.

Progressives admired Young's work and recognized that her popularity among teachers was a tremendous asset to the reform cause. Throughout her career Young was a strong supporter of the right of a teacher to join a union. Many reformers did not understand how important this was to teachers. John Dewey understood and in fact became the first member of the American Federation of Teachers. Young's credibility among teachers was valued even by those who rejected unions.

One point on which Young strongly agreed with Harper was the need to end direct political influence in the schools, particularly in the hiring and firing of teachers. In 1899 she resigned as assistant superintendent of schools to protest continual political interference from the board of education in day-to-day administration.

In that same year she joined the faculty of the University of Chicago's Department of Education. Courageously, she decided to undertake the intellectual demands of obtaining a research-based degree while in her fifties. A year later she received her Ph.D. in education with a dissertation entitled "Isolation in the Schools." Young's willingness and ability to work at this level was typical of the group of women reformers active in Hyde Park, such as Sophonisba Breckinridge and the Abbott sisters, with whom she was closely associated. In many ways they were doing similar work. Breckinridge and the Abbotts broke new ground in social work, both in research and practice. Young wanted to see the same growth in educational practice and in research.

Young returned to the Chicago public schools in 1909 as superintendent and served in that capacity until 1915. By 1909, 67 percent of the children in the public schools were from immigrant families. Young worked to demonstrate that Dewey's ideas could succeed in a large, underfunded system trying to absorb a highly diverse, rapidly growing, and extremely poor student

Ella Flagg Young's pioneering career as both a school administrator and an academic still has few rivals. *(Library of Congress)*

population. Her struggles are familiar today. But the extent to which she was revered by teachers and reformers alike is rare.

*

While Young struggled to improve the schools, progressives lost the battle for city government when Charles Merriam was defeated in the 1911 mayoral election. The reformers' failure to take control of the city left the public schools open to the systematic looting of its resources by corrupt politicians.

Plundering the school system already had a long, sad history in Chicago. The city had received substantial land grants from the federal government earmarked for school use before the first school actually opened, intended to provide a permanent source of funding. Much of this land, including valuable property in the downtown Loop, was sold off in Chicago's early years. The remaining land continued to be leased or sold for less than its value, even after it became clear that the overcrowded, under-funded schools desperately needed money.

Apart from the tragic dissipation of the school lands, public money intended for the schools was often diverted. William Hale Thompson, who defeated Merriam in the mayoral election, openly interfered with the schools in any way he chose. He sold promotions and forced principals to order equipment they did not want at inflated prices from companies controlled by his friends. In one outrageous example of the larceny widespread throughout the system, school furniture turned up in school board members' summer homes. In the 1920s many board members went to prison for corruption. As the Democrats exercised virtual one-party control of the city from the 1930s on, challenging the continuing diversion of money away from schools became more difficult. The depression made it still harder to maintain a system already deeply damaged by corruption. Schools literally ran out of money, and teachers were paid in nearly worthless script.

In 1933 teachers, parents, and community members formed a Save Our Schools Committee in response to devastating cuts in service. Charles Merriam had enjoyed support from the business community when he served as Hyde Park's alderman from 1909 to 1917. Now he tried to rally prominent businessmen to support the committee, but he got no response. Business leaders who supported the Harper Report in a booming economy stepped back in hard times. The committee changed its name to Citizens School Committee and forged ahead, remaining at the center of the fight for reforms for several decades.

William C. Reavis, a University of Chicago professor of education, chaired the committee from 1933 to 1937. Reavis prepared careful reports on the sorry state of the schools. In 1936, for example, he demonstrated that the "business administration" component of Chicago's school costs was 82.9 percent compared to 34 percent in New York and 29 percent in Philadelphia.

In 1947 Reavis warmly supported the appointment of Herold C. Hunt as superintendent. Hunt, who had headed the Kansas City school system, was greeted with hype and high expectations. He did an excellent job and managed to please both the teachers' union and university-based reformers.

Benjamin Willis, the next superintendent appointed in 1953, left a very different legacy. While at the beginning of his tenure he achieved some of the reformers' basic goals—raising teachers' pay and lowering class size—he is primarily remembered as a determined defender of segregation. He was a prodigious builder, and during his tenure Chicago acquired numerous new schools. Their sites were chosen to reinforce segregation: schools were built within black communities to keep the students within these neighborhoods.

Chicago's public schools were well regarded at the time. Many graduates were prepared to enter the expanding college system while others were qualified to begin jobs. Expectations in some areas were lower. For example, handicapped children were often simply not served by the public schools. But general public satisfaction with urban schools was at a level that is hard to imagine today.

Paradoxically the improvements that Hunt and Willis instigated made liberals more eager to open the public schools to black children. Today people talk of the need to rebuild urban schools from the ground up. At this time the city had a strong system, and every expectation was that it would continue to improve. The question was whether black children would be allowed to attend the same schools that white children attended. Strong schools did not have to be built, they would have to be shared.

Some provisions had been made specifically for black students. In 1939 DuSable High School opened on the South Side. Wendell Phillips was already established there as a high-achieving black high school which occupied an imposing building. Wonderfully talented alumni added to Phillips's reputation. The schools were the educational equivalent of the Ida B. Wells housing development: functional, prized by the community, and segregated.

Willis wanted no public discussion of race in regard to the public schools. He claimed he did not know how many black children attended the public schools and that it would be illegal for him to try to find out. He refused to discuss the need to desegregate the schools. Hyde Parkers who had embarked on the integration of their community felt that desegregation of the schools was an urgent priority.

They retaliated against Willis's obstinacy with their favorite weapon: detailed information. In 1964 two University of Chicago professors produced reports on the state of the Chicago schools. Philip M. Hauser, chairman of the Sociology Department, led a team that prepared a report documenting the overwhelming segregation of the schools and the impact of segregation on students. Hauser's study was exactly the one Willis did not want. It demonstrated that black schools were seriously overcrowded more often than white schools. Some were so overcrowded that the students attended school in shifts.

Robert J. Havighurst, a professor of education, produced a lengthy report rivaling William Rainey Harper's in size and depth, on the overall state of Chicago public school education, with numerous, detailed recommendations for change. Both reports stirred controversy, but "the effect . . . on the actual conduct of the schools was negligible," according to Mary Herrick, the leading historian of the Chicago Public Schools.

The consequences of ignoring the recommendations were quite different for the two reports. When the Hauser report was issued, black students were already overrepresented in the public schools, but substantial numbers of white students remained. At the time there was a real opportunity to desegregate the schools. But by the time desegregation was seriously attempted in the late 1980s, too few white students remained in the system to integrate more than a handful of schools. The Havighurst report had a different fate. Many of its ideas, including in-service training for teachers, enhanced status for principals, increased use of technology, and preschool for disadvantaged students, resurfaced and were implemented much later.

In the 1970s and 1980s the schools failed to improve. White students emptied out of the public schools and today constitute about 10 percent of the student population. Many whites moved to the suburbs, but that's not the only explanation. Many white parents who remained in the city enrolled their children in private and parochial schools. Many middle-class black parents made the same choices. Most public school students were now poor minorities who did not meet national norms for achievement.

In 1988 Mayor Richard M. Daley formally assumed control of the Chicago public schools through special state legislation. Increased authority was invested in the superintendent of schools, newly retitled the chief executive officer, to be appointed by the mayor. The school board shrank and became a rubber stamp for the mayor. Some aspects of school reform in Chicago recall Harper's plans, including the small school board and the empowered superintendent. Ironically, Harper sought to reduce the size of the school board in order to reduce political influence on the schools. Given the vast increase in mayoral authority, it turned out that the smaller school board increased direct political influence over the schools.

The pressure for community input was deflected with the creation of a new institution: locally elected councils at every school. These new local councils, composed of the principal, an elected parent, a teacher, and community representatives as well as a student at the high school, have a major role in hiring principals, control the spending of some state and federal dollars, and exercise general advisory powers. Harper would have resisted such a proposal, but the Citizens Schools Committee might have liked the idea. While local school councils have important powers, the fact that they are dispersed among literally hundreds of schools ensures that the councils have no influence on overall policy. At the same time the councils are saddled with the chore of hiring principals—without access to the kinds of personnel files that would be available in any business setting. Not surprisingly, the councils have chosen bad principals as well as good ones. Both the mayor and the CEO of the schools have worked to reduce the councils' authority.

A major motivation for school reform was to improve and professionalize school management, a goal dating back to the progressives. But the new school reformers, including the mayor, look to different professions for leadership. Harper and the educational reformers who came after him sought new professional school administrators, specially trained in scientific educational theory and practice and able to lead the schools to new levels of achievement. Instead the newest reformers recruit leaders with experience in other fields, especially business. This is a major break with the past. Harper may have favored close partnerships with members of the business elite, but he would not have asked them for advice on running the schools.

One consequence of the emphasis on business leadership has been the very limited influence of the University of Chicago on the shaping of the latest round of school reform. The university decided to disband its Department of Education in 1996, citing uneven research quality and the difficulty of rebuilding a strong department.

The university's Center for Urban School Improvement has opened a number of charter schools, but its status is not ahead of other charter school providers. Recently the closest direct connection between the university and the public schools has probably been John Q. Easton, a Hyde Parker and director of the University of Chicago Consortium on School Research. Easton worked for the Chicago Public Schools and is now at the U.S. Department of Education. He does innovative research assessing the effectiveness of instruction and the health of the school climate.

Mayor Richard M. Daley appointed the hard-hitting Paul Vallas, a former city budget director, as the first chief executive officer of the Chicago Public Schools. Vallas's personal style was endlessly disruptive, but he created an atmosphere favorable to change and certainly dramatically increased public expectations about Chicago schools.

His successor was a tall, quiet former basketball star named Arne Duncan. Duncan, a lifelong Hyde Parker, is a graduate of the university's Laboratory Schools and Harvard University. He had never taught or run a school. He had no professional training in education and had never progressed beyond a bachelor's degree. At the same time he had no business background or significant administrative experience either.

But as a person Duncan appealed to many people. He had lived the dream of many American men when he proved himself as a basketball player. He is committed to improving education for poor children but never sounds shrill or self-righteous like so many reform advocates. He has formidable self-control, refuses to be drawn into a shouting match, and disdains personal attacks on those he does not agree with.

Even as a young man, Duncan had an unusual network of personal relationships. His father taught at the University of Chicago while his mother ran an after-school educational enrichment program for poor black children. As a result, Duncan had an uncommonly broad mixture of social contacts. On the one hand, for example, he formed a close friendship with John Rogers, a member of Hyde Park's black elite, who went on to found the hugely successful Ariel Fund. They met and became close friends when both were students at the Laboratory Schools. On the other hand, Duncan grew up with a group of poor black students who attended his mother's program. One of them, Ron Raglin, came to work for Duncan at the public schools. He had grown up in North Kenwood, physically close to Hyde Park but a world away. He told me he regarded Duncan's mother as his second mother.

John Rogers gave Duncan the money to start the Ariel Community Academy, a Chicago public school located in North Kenwood, a black community north of Hyde Park–Kenwood. Rogers's funding allowed the school to employ more teachers than usual and offer after school programming. Test scores improved. The school's success brought Duncan to the attention of Mayor Daley's ally Gerry Chico, and Chico brought Duncan into the central office of the public school system. From there the mayor selected him to be CEO of the schools.

Duncan famously kept his cool in this hot seat. When Obama began his search for an urban school chief to serve as his secretary of education, Duncan was one of the longest-lasting candidates and probably the only one not locked into a major public feud.

Duncan's limitations have been primarily those of content. The public schools do not provide a quality education for all students. By the time they should reach high school, many Chicago children are not in school; far more fail to graduate.

Neither Arne Duncan nor Barack Obama attended or taught in the public schools they are trying to improve, but they share a deep belief in the untapped potential of America's minority children. *(Associated Press)*

Duncan's core ideas—including closing schools, replacing large schools with smaller ones often run by private groups, greater independence for principals, and performance incentives—have not proved substantial enough to produce enough seats in decent schools, especially high schools, to serve all the students who need to be served.

Vallas started and Duncan expanded a new network of high schools that enroll students selectively, based on test scores. This produces some schools with high test scores. In a city as large as Chicago it is not surprising that there are enough high-scoring high school students to fill several modestly sized new high schools. In order words, the pool of high-scoring students has been rearranged, not increased. At the same time the percentage of students actually attending high school has not risen. Incentives for achievement tend to encourage high schools to shed lower-performing students as quickly as possible.

Meanwhile the Chicago school system has become increasingly fragmented and chaotic, all in the name of innovation. One telling fact is that black students are more likely to travel longer distances to high school than they did before, but most attend schools that perform as poorly as the schools they used to attend.

Arne Duncan's ideas are now being tested at the national level. From a Hyde Park perspective, his career is unusual. Earlier reformers in education and related fields often moved on to Washington when their local ambitions were thwarted. By contrast, Duncan was selected to move up to Washington as a popular schools chief who had the mayor's full confidence. Like Obama, Duncan has taken Hyde Park's traditional push for reform down a new, more centrist path. His ability to negotiate the middle ground has propelled him farther than more academically minded Hyde Park reformers were able to go. The results of this strategy are unknown but eagerly anticipated.

Are Hyde Park's own schools good enough to serve as national models? Today the community is home to a variety of public, private, and parochial schools, many of which are strong enough academically to draw students from outside the neighborhood. The University of Chicago's Laboratory Schools are the most famous in the community, but others, including the public high school, Kenwood Academy, are well known within the city.

Other communities have strong public schools. The next question has to be, how racially diverse are Hyde Park's schools? Some are very diverse, some are not. Arne Duncan's daughter attended the Ray elementary school in Hyde Park. Ray does not test students for admission and accepts all students within

The University of Chicago Laboratory Schools emphasized the teaching of foreign languages and an appreciation for other cultures. *(University of Chicago Library, Special Collections Research Center)*

its attendance boundary who choose to attend. Students from outside the boundary may apply to be admitted by lottery to available spaces. The Duncans resided within the attendance boundary.

Hyde Parkers have tried to maintain integrated, high-performing public schools since the neighborhood achieved racial balance. Today there are not enough white and Asian students attending public school in Hyde Park to integrate all its public elementary schools. Ray is one of two Hyde Park elementary schools that remain racially diverse. In 2008–2009 Ray was 21 percent white, 56.4 percent black, 13.5 percent Asian, 8.3 percent Hispanic, and .6 percent Native American. In a system where white students are few, Ray's racial composition was a political godsend for Duncan.

Murray, a language academy launched by parents who wanted to increase good public school options in Hyde Park, is also racially diverse. Murray admits by lottery but does not test for admission.

How did these two schools remain racially diverse? To begin with, they had strong leaders. Sara Spurlark, who is black and has lived in Hyde Park since 1947, served as principal of the Ray school from 1975 until 1989. She remains a beloved authority figure in the neighborhood. Cydney Fields, who is white, succeeded her. Before becoming principal, she had worked with autistic students. Ray has been racially and economically diverse for years. Under Fields's leadership, the last barrier to inclusive education fell and the school became a model for integrating children with special needs into regular classrooms. Murray similarly had principals—particularly Virginia Vaske and Michael Keno—with deep roots in the community who have devoted many years to building the school's reputation.

These effective educational leaders understood that they had to work closely with parents. The people most likely to recruit students for a school successfully when the family has options, are other parents. Parents who throw themselves into networking with other parents and advocate passionately for their schools are a matchless resource for urban educators.

Both Ray and Murray have received major physical plant investments, reflecting years of lobbying by the community, especially by the parents. A politically connected Hispanic parent played a crucial role in securing funds for Ray's annex. The neighborhood wanted enhanced facilities for these two schools because they were academically successful and to help maintain racial diversity. The building additions improved their appearance and added such features as libraries, lunchrooms, conference rooms, and a gym. In an affluent suburb most parents would consider the facilities barely adequate, but in Chicago they are distinctly above the average.

Other public schools in Hyde Park have not been able to achieve racial diversity. The reduction in neighborhood population density and the aging of the remaining population have reduced the pool of students. The University of Chicago offers half-tuition at its Laboratory Schools for students whose parents are university affiliated. Some public school advocates attack this subsidy, arguing that these students are unfairly lost to the public schools. This is not necessarily true; some students eligible for this tuition break attend public school anyway. Families make all sorts of decisions, including using public elementary school and then private high school. Many special-needs children attend public school regardless of their parents' university affiliation. The existence of a private alternative may encourage some families to live in the neighborhood and try using the public schools, knowing they have a private-school alternative to fall back on.

Some of the parents who have worked so hard on behalf of Hyde Park's public schools are connected with the University of Chicago, and some are not. Those who are part of the university community range from graduate students to distinguished professors to staff members. They share a sense that urban public schools can provide a first-rate education and that their children will benefit from learning alongside children who are not just like them.

Over the years Ray and Murray's success has attracted the attention of parents who want to improve the public school options in their neighborhoods. Sara Spurlark, the former principal of Ray, recounts many hours advising groups of parents, particularly from South Shore, an entirely black, mixed-income community south of Hyde Park. She has urged parents to choose an elementary school as a group. If they find a principal they can work with, she suggests, they can transform a local school. "When they told me they wanted Ray School," she recalls, "I told them they could have Ray School on their block." Her advice fell on deaf ears. She did not find the group solidarity or the self-confidence that made Hyde Parkers effective school advocates.

Maintaining economic diversity in a public school is made more difficult because middle-class students are entitled to lower state and federal funding than poor students. Some state and most federal funding is directed at improving education for poor students. The unintended result is that middle-class students cost individual public schools money. Parental fund-raising provides some money for schools that attract middle-class students; but this activity produces far less than what is lost. While parental fund-raising often builds a sense of group purpose and raises morale, it is no substitute for tax dollars.

Thus schools that successfully attract middle-class students and perform well on standardized tests lack sufficient funds to lower class size and provide additional programming. Both Ray and Murray fall into this category and have larger classes than most other Chicago public schools. This is partly because many parents push hard to get their children into a high-performing school, but it also reflects the fact that these schools lack the funds other schools use to reduce class size.

If maintaining a racially and economically diverse elementary school is difficult, maintaining the same balance at the high school level is still harder. In the 1960s, black migration on the South Side meant that Hyde Park High School, actually located in nearby Woodlawn, became entirely black. After much debate the community decided to launch a new high school rather than attempt to integrate Hyde Park High School.

In 1966 the new Kenwood Academy high school began by holding classes in an old elementary school. A new building was built for the high school, the largest investment in public educa-

An early photo (circa 1896) from the William H. Ray elementary school includes a few black students. *(University of Chicago Library, Special Collections Research Center)*

tion made in the community since urban renewal. In 1970 the first senior class graduated from this brand-new building. The new Kenwood Academy building looked very suburban, but the funding provided fell far short of suburban standards.

Kenwood opened with a majority of black students but a substantial minority of white students. The school offered a wide array of courses, the most available in any Chicago public high school. The academically challenging program attracted high-performing students of both races. Top students had the opportunity to take regularly scheduled University of Chicago classes. In the late 1990s a combination of poor school leadership and new possibilities in selective-enrollment high schools emptied Kenwood of most of its white students, many high-scoring black students, and some of its better-known faculty.

Since then Kenwood has reestablished itself under a particularly able principal, Elizabeth Kirby. She is often cited by Arne Duncan as the kind of leader he is seeking for urban high schools. She exemplifies the best of the new principals. She earned a bachelor's degree in urban studies at Harvard, a master's degree in social science at the University of Chicago, and trained as a principal under the respected New Leaders for New Schools program.

John Q. Easton has developed a means of assessing whether high school freshmen are "on track" to graduate, a crucial determination in a school system where half the entering freshmen fail to graduate. Easton reports that no high school in Chicago has worked more effectively than Kenwood to implement an "on track" program. Kenwood now has an on-track rate of more than 80 percent, an astonishing success for a school that admits only half its students selectively and has a high poverty rate.

Hyde Park's public schools have maintained a focus on integration and diversity. The schools have provided excellent, free education on a shoestring budget. And they have reflected Hyde Park's unique culture. In one example, one of Ray's fifth-grade classes produced its own dramatic version of the epic of *Gilgamesh*, the story of the ancient Sumerian hero. William Rainey Harper would have approved the subject matter, and John Dewey would have applauded how the children structured their own learning experience. I watched the performance as the narrator, aged eleven, intoned solemnly that the townspeople of the ancient city had offended the powerful god Marduk. Therefore Marduk sent the Great Bull of Heaven to destroy their city. A young girl, trying to hold a stern expression on her face, dashed across the stage wearing a bright red, horned, plastic Chicago Bulls cap and red T-shirt. The audience of parents and grandparents roared with delight. The children reminded the academics among them to wear their learning lightly and not forget to laugh.

EIGHT
OBAMA IN HYDE PARK

Barack Obama was the first black candidate for president nominated by a major party. Hyde Park provided him with white neighbors but not at the expense of losing black neighbors. The neighborhood afforded Obama a nearly unique racial setting. When he entered a local elementary school to vote on November 5, 2008, he was not a black man living in a black neighborhood, or a black man living in a white neighborhood. Both scenarios would have been awkward reminders of racial divisions in the United States. Instead Obama voted from an integrated neighborhood, home to blacks, whites, and Asians for more than forty years. That the neighborhood provided him with such a helpful and reassuring base was not just a happy accident.

Hyde Park has a nearly unique status as a stable integrated community. Obama has written movingly of the poor black communities he represented while serving in the Illinois State Senate between 1997 and 2004. Because of Hyde Park–Kenwood's racial composition, from the start of his political career he also represented whites, Asians, and well-to-do blacks. His early supporters were as diverse as his first cabinet choices.

The neighborhood itself decided to embrace integration more than sixty years ago. A major community grassroots organizing effort was followed by a massive, publicly funded urban renewal program. The racially balanced community that resulted was small but in a key location near downtown Chicago, on the lakefront, and encompassing a rich cultural environment.

Before achieving a racial balance, the community had already become a center of reform politics. Progressive politicians, including scholars and women, sought more influence in Chicago from a base in Hyde Park. The neighborhood's liberal political agenda offered an alternative for people throughout Chicago who were dissatisfied with corrupt patronage politics. Hyde Parkers challenged machine politics and, when thwarted within the city, took their case to Washington.

In the 1960s Hyde Park reformers realized their goals required progressive black leadership. They looked for strong black leaders to serve a liberal white constituency as well as the black community. Their willingness to rally around Harold Washington helped him become Chicago's first black mayor and a mayor committed to reform.

In his early memoir *Dreams from My Father*, Obama describes how he worked as a community organizer in Roseland, a poor black community south of Hyde Park–Kenwood. The two communities gave him very different opportunities. Roseland educated him about the human side of efforts to end poverty and provided him with street credentials. Hyde Park, on the other hand, was his political incubator and then his launching pad.

In 1985 Roseland was the entirely black neighborhood Hyde Park–Kenwood might have become if community organizing and urban renewal had not intervened. Originally Roseland had been an attractive, largely white, working-class neighborhood. After racially restrictive real estate convenants were struck down, blacks began to buy in Roseland. Obama emphasizes the speed of racial transformation: "Entire blocks turned over in less than six months; entire neighborhoods in less than five years." In 1965 Roseland had had a majority of white residents; by 1975 it was uniformly black. Obama judges further that although the community "never fully recovered from this racial upheaval," individual black home owners were pleased with the improvement in circumstances they gained by moving to Roseland.

Roseland continued to be a desirable place for working families. But the neighborhood was hit with a series of successive shocks. Massive job losses occurred when industries left Chicago. Anchor institutions, including banks and other businesses, moved or disappeared. Moreover Roseland, unlike Hyde Park–Kenwood, included large public housing projects that deteriorated and became a major liability for the neighborhood. Obama worked in one of these public housing projects called Altgeld Gardens, trying to organize tenants.

In 1983 Harold Washington's election as mayor of Chicago brought new hope to Roseland. But new openness in government and a fairer sharing of the city's resources did not bring the changes Roseland needed. Public housing and the public schools in particular continued to decline.

Obama worked on the ground to improve conditions in Roseland. He looked for self-interest as the motivation for people to join in his organizing efforts. He interviewed community members, attempting to find out what issue would galvanize them. Saul Alinsky, a graduate of the University of Chicago, pioneered this model of community organizing. In the 1930s Alinsky organized in the Back of the Yards community where Mary McDowell had worked. But focusing on self-interest did not always help Obama's organizing efforts. He lost some of his best allies when they decided that their families would be best served by moving to a different neighborhood.

There is no trace of Alinsky's confrontational style or his contempt for political parties in Obama's thinking. Alinsky was a radical. Obama was willing to try Alinsky's methods but was not influenced to become a radical himself.

It is interesting to compare Hyde Park–Kenwood's block clubs of the early 1950s and the organizations Obama tried to foster in Roseland. In Roseland women took leadership roles, at first reluctantly, and enjoyed their new sense of power. Women were also often leaders in the Hyde Park block groups. Obama was a paid organizer. The Hyde Park groups similarly employed smart young men as organizers.

The working- and lower-middle-class blacks who rarely felt comfortable in the Hyde Park–Kenwood block clubs provided leadership for similar groups in Roseland. Probably these blacks did not follow better-educated blacks into community organizations in Hyde Park–Kenwood because they sensed they were near the bottom of the social totem pole. In Roseland, however, these classes of blacks, particularly home owners, were at the top of the social ladder and provided valuable leadership. Indeed the block club model remains widespread in lower-middle- and working-class black neighborhoods today. Homemade signs often welcome visitors to an individual block in Chicago while reciting a list of "rules," precisely capturing the "dual sense of individual advancement and collective decline" that Obama notes in Roseland.

What were the real consequences of Obama's community organizing efforts for Roseland? They did help focus attention on people's needs. Unlike top-down policy efforts, community organizing highlights what people identify as their needs, not what others think they are. The people Obama worked with were often pillars of their community, and their voices deserved to be heard.

His limited success as an organizer reflected his constituency. Unlike Hyde Parkers, people in Roseland did not command lawmakers' attention. The institutions they supported—local school and churches, for example—did not have the influence to win substantial government financial support.

Roseland still struggles with the problems Obama tried to address as well as new challenges created by the current recession and sub-prime lending fiasco. Most troubling of all, the community is wracked by youth violence. In September 2009 a student was beaten to death in front of Fenger High School, a public school in Roseland, drawing national attention.

After working as an organizer, Obama left Chicago to attend Harvard Law School. He graduated in 1991, having attracted widespread attention as the first black editor-in-chief of the *Law Review*. Judson Minor, a politically savvy Chicago lawyer, recruited Obama for his firm, at that time known as Davis, Minor, and Barnhill. Although Minor was one of hundreds of people interested in hiring Obama, he succeeded because of the kind of opportunity he could offer. His firm may be as unique among law firms as Hyde Park is among neighborhoods. Minor founded the firm with Allison Davis, the son of the University of Chicago's first black professor whose name was also Alison Davis. The partners built a reputation for their civil rights work and their social conscience. At the same time they did not run a legal aid office. The firm's lawyers tried to win cases and earn fees. Obama was thus able to make a wonderful compromise.

He did not have to join a large, prestigious law firm where he would have made more money but the firm would have owned 110 percent of his time. Nor did he have to follow his social justice ideals into poorly paid legal aid or advocacy work.

The choice was inspired for another less obvious reason: Judson Minor has an unequaled track record of working with and supporting reform-minded minority politicians. For example, his firm repeatedly sued the City of Chicago for approving revised ward maps that unfairly increased white representation on the City Council. And the suits were successful, thereby increasing minority representation on the council.

Obama chose to live in Hyde Park and stayed there until he moved to the White House. The neighborhood offered him several advantages. To begin with, a well-educated black man is not an anomaly in Hyde Park. Some notable ones lived and worked in the neighborhood, and the memory of exemplary past figures still lingers.

Dual religious, racial, or ethnic identity is common in Hyde Park. Marriages across religious, racial, and ethnic lines have not raised eyebrows for decades. People of mixed heritage often need time to sort out their own identity. Many Hyde Parkers sympathize with Obama's personal journey, beginning at his mother's detachment from sectarian religion and ending at his membership in the Reverend Jeremiah Wright's Trinity Church.

Finally, many residents of Hyde Park had experienced a childhood that included exile or long stays in other countries for scholarly or other professional reasons. Valerie Jarrett, who became a close adviser to Obama, was born in Iran where her father practiced medicine. Many people would understand the sense of isolation or dislocation that can be a part of growing up "different" from the rest of community. At the same time Hyde Parkers tend to value such experiences and even seek them out for themselves and their children.

Obama's family home in Hyde Park is one of many large homes in the area, this one most notable for its inhabitants. *(AP Photo/Jerry Lai)*

In 1992 Obama married Michelle Robinson, who had grown up near Hyde Park. In the years following their marriage, Michelle and Barack's personal and professional lives grew more deeply enmeshed in the neighborhood. Remaining in Hyde Park kept them close to Michelle's mother, many relatives, and childhood friends, strengthening these ties as they became the parents of two daughters. At the same time Hyde Park–Kenwood offered both Obamas new professional opportunities. Michelle went to work for the University of Chicago and assumed a leadership role in community organizations; Barack entered politics.

Obama's mother, Ann Dunham, was white and academically talented. She was enraptured with other cultures, idealistically seeking the best in communities very different from her own. Dunham earned a doctorate in anthropology. She married first a fellow student from Kenya and then a man from Indonesia. Each marriage produced one child. Dunham lived for many years in other countries, sometimes with her children in tow.

She produced a long, unpublished thesis (later published post-humously as a book), but an early death from cancer cut short her academic career.

Great emphasis has been placed on Obama's choice of a black wife and a black church. This is seen as an attempt to distance himself from his mother's world. But Hyde Park is his mother's world. She could have easily moved unnoticed in the neighborhood, another anthropologist who married people from the other cultures that fascinated her. The children of such marriages are not suspect in Hyde Park. They are considered privileged to have personal connections that will help them understand other cultures. Quite a few Hyde Parkers do exactly the kind of work Dunham did, with similar goals, while nearly all Hyde Parkers respect such a career.

Although few blacks teach at the University of Chicago or attend it, an important black elite flourishes in Hyde Park–Kenwood. This elite nurtured Obama's career in crucial ways. They mentored him and provided him with access to money and power. Before moving to Chicago, Obama became a high-achieving young black man with no important support from any black people. In Hyde Park he benefited from the friendship and guidance of black people who had made the transition from high-achieving young person with potential to powerful partici-pant in the white worlds of government, finance, real estate, and business. He taught part time at the University of Chicago Law School, located in the neighborhood. He wrote, "I loved the law school classroom" and likened his mission of teaching the Con-stitution to the work of theology professors on the same campus.

Obama used Hyde Park as a mental gymnasium. He liked to discuss issues with people who had strong and often oppos-ing points of view. He stayed fit as a debater, but he did not share his personal beliefs on controversial subjects like the death penalty, the Middle East, or abortion. That was unusual in a neighborhood where people's political beliefs are often clear from the slogans on their T-shirts. In retrospect his reticence seems prescient.

In much the same way, Obama never showed an interest in becoming either an analyst or an advocate in print. He read widely, and he wrote a very personal memoir. Many Hyde Parkers have a cache of unpublished essays and articles and appear in print when and where they can. Obama stayed aloof.

When he decided to enter politics, skilled people were ready and willing to help him. Hyde Park was ready for Barack Obama as a political contender even before he was ready to assume that role. The community did all it could to act as his political support system.

No one in Hyde Park considered his impressive education a barrier or deterrent to a political career. Both black and white politicians from Hyde Park and nearby communities were often well educated and sometimes real scholars. This was true of black politicians whom Hyde Parkers respected, like Earl Dickerson (University of Chicago Law School, alderman), Richard Newhouse (University of Chicago Law School, state senator), and Harold Washington (Northwestern Law School, mayor of Chicago); those they detested, like William Dawson (Northwestern Law School, congressman); and those who broke their hearts, like Carol Moseley Braun (University of Chicago Law School, U.S. Senate).

By Hyde Park's standards, Obama was well educated but not a scholar. He resembled Leon Despres, the intellectual and independent Hyde Park alderman who sparred with the first Mayor Daley. Despres, like Obama, wrote only memoirs. By contrast, Paul Douglas, a U.S. senator and major economist, wrote substantial academic works.

Hyde Parkers worried that Obama would be impeded by Richard M. Daley's powerful presence in Chicago politics.

Daley discourages and undermines any politician who might someday be a viable candidate for mayor. But Obama made his peace early with Daley. He carefully proceeded from the State Senate to the U.S. Senate without ever opposing Daley's wishes.

But in order to begin his political career in Hyde Park, he needed the support of some of Daley's critics. When Obama decided to run for the State Senate in 1995, his earliest supporters included Alan and Lois Dobry, longtime determined opponents of Daley. The Dobrys were ardent supporters of independent politicians like Despres. Alan had rendered crucial service to Harold Washington when he became Chicago's first black mayor. Both Dobrys worked hard on Obama's first campaign for the Illinois Senate. As experienced political street fighters, they knocked out the nominating petitions of Obama's opponents, thus guaranteeing his victory. Obama benefited from skills that others honed in fighting Daley, but he never embraced opposition to Daley.

The decision not to oppose Daley caused concern in Hyde Park. Many Hyde Parkers, especially older residents, think that Hyde Park politicians exist to oppose any mayor named Daley. Some of them forgave Obama when he won the presidential election, and some did not.

The Dobrys are Jewish, like many of the Hyde Parkers who helped Obama in his early political career. Even David Axelrod, one of his most important advisers, has a Hyde Park connection. He studied at the University of Chicago, wrote for the local newspaper, and married a woman who grew up in Hyde Park, the daughter of a well-known doctor. When right-wing bloggers tire of the socialists-for-Obama conspiracy, tracking the Jews-for-Obama conspiracy can easily occupy their time.

But not all his crucial early support came from Jews. State Representative Barbara Flynn Currie, a lifelong Hyde Parker,

Obama getting a haircut at his regular barbershop in Hyde Park—a man comfortable in his urban village. *(David Katz)*

gave Obama invaluable assistance in his early campaigns, including his very first race for the State Senate. The seat he sought had opened up when the incumbent state senator, Alice Palmer, decided to run for a vacant seat in the U.S. House of Representatives. After Palmer was defeated in a special election by Jesse Jackson, Jr., she announced that she would run again for her State Senate seat. She clearly expected Obama to step aside for her. Currie and Alderman Toni Preckwinkle supported the relatively unknown Obama when he stuck to his guns and remained in the race, which he won.

Some Hyde Parkers also feared that Obama would self-destruct and succumb to bribery, corruption, or worse. "I have had my heart broken so many times," says Abner Mikva, former congressman, federal judge, presidential adviser, and the dean of Hyde Park Democrats. The list of promising black politicians who came to bad ends goes back to the 1960s. Hyde Parkers had high hopes for Fred Hubbard, an independent black alderman from the nearby Second Ward, first elected in 1969. Hubbard was a University of Chicago–educated social worker who founded the Independent Peoples' Organization to bring the benefits of independent politics to the black community. His career ended in disgrace after he stole money. Later Hyde Parkers looked to Mel Reynolds, a brilliant young congressman whose career was ended by his conviction on charges of sexual misconduct and obstruction of justice. Mikva recalls Al Raby, a civil rights activist who served as Harold Washington's campaign manager during his first successful run for mayor. Raby died without achieving elective office.

Meanwhile Obama used the State Senate as a moot court, learning the legislative ropes. He built relationships and arranged compromises. He developed a close working relationship with the president of the senate, Emil Jones. Hyde Parkers continued to watch his back as best they could.

In his later years Abner Mikva returned to Hyde Park and became a close friend and adviser to Obama. When Obama was harshly criticized for missing an important vote in the State Senate, Obama explained that his daughter had become ill while traveling, delaying the family's return to Illinois. Mikva wrote to the *Herald*, Hyde Park's community newspaper, "I spent 20 years in elective office, most of them representing Hyde Park. . . . The most difficult conflict . . . was the responsibility to be and do what the public expected and still try to be a good father and husband." His letter proved an effective defense.

Barack Obama was clearly inspired by Harold Washington's inclusive vision. But he learned early on in his career that the old ethnic politics were alive and well in Chicago. In 2000 he challenged Congressman Bobby Rush in the Democratic primary for his seat in the U.S. House of Representatives. Rush represented an overwhelmingly black district on the South Side of Chicago that included Hyde Park. He began his career as a member of the militant Black Panthers organization and went on to serve as a pro-Washington alderman in Chicago's City Council. Rush never bothered to conceal his low opinion of whites, women, or Hyde Parkers.

Mayor Richard M. Daley was pleased with Obama's decision as Rush had run for mayor against Daley in 1999. Hyde Parkers, many of whom despised being represented by Rush, rejoiced. An articulate, well-educated young black man who shared their values would end Rush's career. They prematurely planned victory parties.

Rush scoffed at Obama's Harvard education. He always referred to Obama as "the professor," echoing mockery directed at Charles Merriam and Paul Douglas, University of Chicago professors who had served on the Chicago City Council decades earlier. Rush coupled these attacks with the claim that Obama was too close to "them" to be one of "us." Them, of course, referred to Hyde Parkers, black and white alike.

Obama began as a reluctant campaigner. Somewhere during the course of this contest he overcame his distaste for the glad-handing side of politics. Nonetheless Bobby Rush handed Obama his only defeat, which was probably a gift in disguise.

Hyde Parkers could not help Obama achieve a comfort level with working-class whites. Few of them possess that asset. Unlike many of the black politicians who preceded him, Obama gained no credibility with white working-class voters by serving in the military. Besides Dickerson and Dawson, those who served in the armed forces include Newhouse, Metcalfe, and Washington. Bobby Rush served in the army until he went AWOL. Not surprisingly, black women politicians, including Carol Moseley Braun, did not serve. Obama was left without a potent defense against charges of lacking patriotism, and he had no means of connecting with white working-class voters, who became a difficult constituency for him.

When his book *The Audacity of Hope* scored a financial success in 2006, Obama moved his family to a large house in Kenwood. Although the new house was located only a few blocks from their previous home, the two differed greatly in style and setting. The large, detached, stately homes on oversized lots in South Kenwood are not available in Hyde Park. South Kenwood has appealed for decades to successful professionals who want to enjoy suburban space and privacy without leaving the city. Thus Obama followed a well-worn path traveled by numerous other aspiring young people, both black and white.

Hyde Park did not have the political talent to get Obama to the U.S. Senate, let alone the White House. As his career gained momentum, his staff included new people with no connections to the neighborhood. Hyde Parkers, with the exception of close advisers like Valerie Jarrett, were relegated to the cheering section. They had never been happier. More than 97 percent of them voted for him in November 2008.

One Hyde Parker who has stayed close to Obama as he transitioned to the White House is twenty-eight-year-old David Katz. Katz served as Obama's special assistant during his 2004 Senate campaign in Illinois and during much of his tenure in Washington as a junior senator. The two became particularly close while weaving through the cornfields of rural Illinois to visit farmers and everyday citizens, catching brief naps at motels along the way. Obama's chief strategist, David Axelrod, once referred to their travels as "Katz and Obama's Excellent Adventure." Katz is also a professional photographer and has served as the president's personal photographer, most recently during the 2008 election. He now works in Washington as special assistant to energy secretary Steven Chu, leading the department's pubic campaign to promote energy efficiency.

Katz's father, Norm, was a real estate developer who was one of the first to develop residential housing within Chicago's Loop. Katz's mother, Lucinda, is Chinese American and was a popular director of the University of Chicago's Laboratory Schools. For many years Lucinda was a Hyde Park celebrity, easily recognized and often greeted, solicited, or hassled by eager parents as she made her way through the neighborhood. She had a gift for handling ambitious mothers and fathers. Hyde Parkers like to tell the story that when the Katzes moved into their first home in Hyde Park, they discovered that the family next door was also a Jewish-Chinese blend. That's Hyde Park, people would remark, rather complacently.

Obama is in a sense bigger than Hyde Park. He no longer has to step carefully to avoid some of Hyde Park's silly, unending local disputes. Now he deals with war and economic disaster. But Hyde Park provided him with a unique set of circumstances. He could exercise his mind in a place that challenged his thinking. He could live in a world that felt like his mother's while rejoicing in the company of a black wife and the support of a black church with unusual intellectual standards. He could learn how to move confidently as a talented black person in a white world, from people whose families had been doing just that for several generations.

Hyde Parkers were waiting for him before he undertook his political quest. The neighborhood offered him an opportunity to lead, and he seized it. The neighborhood supported him in a range of ways, from money to skills to useful insights. But the self-discipline and the reticence that allowed him to make use of the amazing opening that happened for him were his before he ever saw Hyde Park.

As Obama is judged during his presidency, Hyde Park will be judged. How helpful is the neighborhood's understanding of community, progress, and reform? In a real way, Obama's ascent is an opportunity for Hyde Park to showcase its ideals and its values, but it also creates a risk.

Hyde Parkers' own political agenda is often farther to the left than Obama's. The contribution Hyde Park made to his career was not the inculcation of left-wing doctrines. It provided a culture of opportunity. Its contribution was to foster a highly talented young politician's desire to lead the entire American community. This support grew out of work and ideas that reach back more than a hundred years.

Hyde Park is a self-confident community entitled to be proud of its strengths. The jury is out as to how proud Hyde Park will be of Obama's presidency. But the community prepared him for his opportunity.

A NOTE ON SOURCES

I received a great deal of help from other Hyde Parkers with particular areas of expertise. Stephen Treffman, archivist emeritus of the Hyde Park Historical Society, generously shared with me his unpublished research into the history of the Palace of Fine Arts building and directed me to Andrew Yox's spirited *Hyde Park Politics, 1861–1919*, published privately by the Historical Society in 1980. Charles Thurow, executive director of the Hyde Park Art Center, sent me a copy of the center's privately published history, which appeared in 1976. Michal Safar, the Hyde Park Historical Society's current archivist, helped me locate photographs.

Raymond Lodato of the National Opinion Research Center allowed me to use portions of his unpublished research into

Richard M. Daley's relationship with black Chicagoans. Alderman Toni Preckwinkle dug out her master's thesis on William Dawson for my use.

Robert Mason, longtime director of the South East Chicago Commission, arranged for me to consult the commission's files on urban renewal at the University of Chicago's Regenstein Library.

Hyde Park's current economic diversity is documented *in A Kaleidoscope of Culture: Measuring the Diversity of Chicago's Neighborhoods*, a study by Lauren Fischer and Joseph P. Schwieterman, published by the Chaddick Institute for Metropolitan Development of De Paul University in July 2008.

Carl Condit provides an incisive account of the construction of the University of Chicago campus in his *Chicago, 1910–1929: Building, Planning, and Urban Technology* (Chicago, 1973). Condit also analyzes the rich symbolism contained in the architectural detail.

Steven Diner's thoughtful *A City and Its Universities: Public Policy in Chicago, 1892–1919* (Chapel Hill, 1980) offers an excellent account of the University of Chicago's early years and its involvement in major policy debates. Diner's book is a model for the intelligent consideration of the role of academics in policymaking. His detailed research into progressive Hyde Parkers is enlightening.

Louis P. Cain helpfully outlines the economic issues around annexation in his article "To Annex or Not? A Tale of Two Towns: Evanston and Hyde Park," in *Economic Explorations*, January 1983, 58–72.

Paul Kroty's *Frank Lloyd Wright and Midway Gardens* (Urbana, Ill., 1998) is the definitive work on this astonishing project.

Several volumes in the Heritage of Sociology Series, which my father, Morris Janowitz, edited, helped me track changes in academic thinking about race, especially *The Social Fabric of the Metropolis*, edited by James F. Short (Chicago, 1971), and *E. Franklin Frazier on Race Relations*, edited by G. Franklin Edwards (Chicago, 1968).

Peter Ascoli has written the only recent biography of his grandfather: *Julius Rosenwald: The Man Who Built Sears, Roebuck and Advanced the Cause of Black Education in the American South* (Bloomington, Ind., 2006). The book is a labor of love and includes a great deal of valuable information. M. R. Werner's *Julius Rosenwald: The Life of a Practical Humanitarian* (New York, 1939) provides interesting contemporary comments on his political involvement, especially in Charles Merriam's mayoral campaign. I was fortunate that while I was learning about Rosenwald, the exhibition *A Force for Change: African-American Art and the Julius Rosenwald Fund* was on display at the Spertus Museum in Chicago. This exploration of Rosenwald's work and vision, expertly curated by Daniel Shulman, brilliantly demonstrated the extent and depth of his influence. The catalogue of the exhibit is a valuable resource.

Barry Karl's *Charles E. Merriam and the Study of Politics* (Chicago, 1974) is the only scholarly biography of a major Hyde Park politician. As the title suggests, it focuses on Merriam's contribution to political science but provides a helpful account of his political career. Merriam's own *Chicago: A More Intimate View of Urban Politics* (Chicago, 1929) remains fascinating reading, especially on the substance of his aldermanic career.

Mary McDowell, Neighbor by Howard E. Wilson (Chicago, 1928) introduces her ideas and allows us to see how her contemporaries viewed her work.

Paul H. Douglas wrote an extensive, highly readable memoir, *In the Fullness of Time* (New York, 1972). Roger Biles has written a helpful analysis of Douglas's Senate career in "Paul H. Douglas, McCarthyism, and the Senatorial Election of 1954," *Journal of the Illinois State Historical Society*, Spring 2002.

Robert Merriam is the missing man in published accounts of Hyde Park's political history, often referred to but not studied in depth.

Hyde Park's special and often stormy political relationship with the City of Chicago comes vividly to life in Adam Cohen and Elizabeth Taylor's *American Pharaoh: Mayor Richard J. Daley, His Battle for Chicago and the Nation* (New York, 2000). This major study sheds light on Robert Merriam's career and even more on Leon Despres's importance for the city as a whole.

An equally valuable resource on the early history of black politics is St. Clair Drake and Horace R. Cayton's *Black Metropolis: A Study of Negro Life in a Northern City* (Chicago, 1945; subsequent editions 1962, 1970). Richard Wright's original introduction is a startling love song in praise of urban sociology. William Grimshaw's useful *Bitter Fruit: Black Politics and the Chicago Machine, 1931–1991* (Chicago, 1992) brings contemporary scholarship to bear on black political history.

Unlike his rival William Dawson, Earl Dickerson is the subject of a full-length biography: *Earl B. Dickerson: A Voice for Freedom and Equality* by Robert J. Blakely and Marcus Shepard (Evanston, Ill., 2006). It includes interviews with colleagues and friends. Leon Despres's memoirs, written with Kenan Heise, *Challenging the Daley Machine: A Chicago Alderman's Memoir* (Evanston, Ill., 2005), offers interesting commentary. The book includes a wonderful 1972 introduction of Despres by Mike Royko, the well-known journalist, and a revealing 1966 article from *Negro Digest* by David Llorens entitled "The Lone 'Negro' Spokesman in Chicago's City Council."

Julia Abrahamson's *A Neighborhood Finds Itself* (New York, 1959) is difficult to read because of its syrupy tone but contains valuable assessments of community action. Written by the first executive director of the Hyde Park–Kenwood Community

Conference soon after urban renewal commenced, it captures the spirit of the period. *The Politics of Urban Renewal: The Chicago Findings*, by Peter H. Rossi and Robert A. Dentier with the assistance of Nelson W. Polsby (New York, 1961) is a detailed study of the Hyde Park experience. *The Impact of Urban Renewal on Small Business: The Hyde Park–Kenwood Case*, by Brian J. L. Berry, Sandra J. Parson, and Rutherford H. Platt (Chicago, 1968), carefully analyzes one aspect of urban renewal. Irving Cutler's *The Jews of Chicago: From Shtetl to Suburb* (Urbana, Ill., 1996) provides useful facts about the Jewish community in Hyde Park and in nearby communities.

In *Making the Second Ghetto: Race and Housing in Chicago, 1940–1960* (Chicago, 1983; rev. ed. 1998], Arnold Hirsch did valuable work in analyzing patterns of racial violence in Chicago related to housing integration that have not received the attention they deserve. But his claim that the integration of Hyde Park–Kenwood contributed to the creation of the vast new ghettos on Chicago's West and South Sides convinced me he is too angry to think clearly on the subject.

Florence Hamlish Levinsohn's *Harold Washington: A Political Biography* (Chicago, 1983) reflects their friendship. Her account is clear, readable, and evokes the spirit of Washington's years at Roosevelt University and his early political work. Levinsohn also conducted a lengthy, revealing interview with Fifth Ward alderman Larry Bloom on the eve of his mayoral campaign, reported as "Lawrence Bloom for Mayor," *Chicago Reader*, October 28, 1988.

My account of the Chicago Public Schools rests firmly on the work of Mary J. Herrick. Her classic study *The Chicago Schools: A Social and Political History* (Beverly Hills, Calif., 1971) is a remarkable work of sound scholarship, enlivened by dry wit. The fact that it is not required reading for the current crop of educational reformers, let alone even in print, reveals a foolish disregard for history that contributes to a myopic reliance on short-term thinking.

John L. Roury reviewed the dismal history of desegregation in Chicago's public schools in "Race, Space, and the Politics of Chicago's Public Schools: Benjamin Willis and the Tragedy of Urban Education," *History of Education Quarterly*, vol. 39, no. 2 (Summer 1999), 117–142.

INDEX

A NOTE ON THE AUTHOR

Rebecca Janowitz lives in the Hyde Park house she grew up in, and raised her own children there. After graduating from the University of Sussex, she studied law at Loyola University, Chicago, and then practiced in a small firm for almost twenty years. Since then she has been active in politics and community affairs—with the South East Chicago Commission, in the Fourth Ward office of Alderman Toni Preckwinkle, with Arne Duncan at the Chicago Public Schools, and most recently at the Cook County Jail. She is the daughter of the late distinguished University of Chicago sociologist Morris Janowitz.